HOOP

muses

FOR
EVERYONE
WHO HAS
LOVED THIS
GAME

HOOP muses

AN INSIDER'S GUIDE TO POP CULTURE AND THE (WOMEN'S) GAME

WRITTEN BY **KATE FAGAN**

CURATED BY **SEIMONE AUGUSTUS**

ILLUSTRATED BY **SOPHIA CHANG**
AND OTHERS

12
TWELVE
NEW YORK BOSTON

CONTENTS

FINAL SCENE: THE RETURN   250

THE FUTURE...

JACKLYN JONES
DING!!
Hi...
Are you lost?
No, I don't believe so. Perhaphs you are?
You must be here for tonight's half time celebration?
You know who you remind me of?
You remind me of a young Maya Moore – oh goodness could she play!
Who?
Oh, child, you don't know Maya Moore? Oh, no, no, no. This cannot stand.
How about a little trip?
We'll have you back by tip-off. I promise.

THE FUTURE

ARTWORK BY MILAN ABAD

NEW YORK, 2072 ⚡ Jacklyn Jones is the best basketball player in the world. Everyone agrees. The media is constantly arguing about all kinds of topics: did agreeing to play the Washington Mystics on Mars in 2070 cost the Seattle Storm that year's title? Are the Los Angeles Sparks the greatest franchise in the WNBA's seventy-five-year history? But Jacklyn's dominance...that's universally agreed upon. She can dunk with either hand. And her outside shot—well, nobody's seen anything like her range and smoothness.

Jacklyn *is* the future. Which is especially relevant on this night, as the league honors its past: the New York Liberty are playing the Phoenix Mercury on the eve of the WNBA's seventy-fifth anniversary. Jacklyn just signed a $100 million contract extension with her hometown team, the Liberty. It's the first nine-figure deal in WNBA history. So, while the greats of the game will converge on sold-out Madison Square Garden for the star-studded event, all eyes will still be on Jacklyn. She's used to it. It's been like this since she was thirteen years old, when she would take her coach's Aeromobil X—the self-flying model—to play showcases across the country.

Inside the Liberty locker room, Jacklyn is sitting alone. She's early; it's still hours before tip-off. She's turned off all notifications to her wrist chip, seeking just a moment of quiet and clarity before the arena begins filling. She takes a deep breath, but as she exhales, a long chime cuts through the silence. She knows what the sound means: someone has entered. She assumes one of her teammates had the same idea she did: a moment of solitude before the madness.

Jacklyn keeps her eyes closed. Then, slowly, reluctantly, she opens them.

Standing in front of her is a stranger, and for a beat Jacklyn is uneasy. How did this woman get inside? But then Jacklyn realizes the woman is older, much older, and seemingly no threat at all. Maybe she's lost? The woman's hair is dark, contrasted against a bright orange hoodie that features a symbol Jacklyn doesn't recognize, but that vaguely reminds her of the current WNBA logo.

"Hi," Jacklyn says tentatively. "Are you lost?"

The woman smiles and says, "No, I don't believe so. Perhaps you are?"

Ah. Jacklyn puts the pieces together. "You must be here for tonight's halftime celebration?" Maybe there was an usher outside she could call, who could help this woman find her way.

"You know who you remind me of?" the woman says, pulling a phone from her pocket. Jacklyn stares at the device. She's only seen one of these—the iPhone, they once called it—in a museum. Jacklyn can't imagine having to use your hands to communicate; so cumbersome. The woman continues, "You remind me of a young Maya Moore—oh, goodness, could she play!"

Jacklyn is confused, and before she can stop herself, she says, "Who?"

The woman's eyes fly to Jacklyn's, and for a moment they stare at each other. The woman squints and says, "Oh, child, you don't know Maya Moore? Oh, no, no, no. This cannot stand." She glances down at the artifact in her hand, and Jacklyn notices the screen is lit up. She's never seen a working iPhone before! How fascinating...

"How about a little trip?" the woman says, raising one eyebrow. She looks down again at her phone, hits a button, then looks up and says, "We'll have you back by tip-off, I promise."

NAISMITH

INVENTOR
OF BASKET BALL?

Details from the winter of 1891, as outlined in journals and newspapers at the time, seem to tell the simple and compelling story of the origin of basket ball. A man named James Naismith,[†] then thirty years old and working at the Springfield (Massachusetts) YMCA and Springfield College, was asked by his boss to create an indoor game to keep his rowdy (male, of course) students engaged during the winter months—you know, between the outdoor seasons of football and baseball.

On the morning of December 12, 1891, Naismith mounted peach baskets[*] on either side of the indoor space and posted on the wall the thirteen rules he had devised. He watched as his physical education students entered the gym and began reading:

1. *The ball may be thrown in any direction with one or both hands.*

2. *The ball may be batted in any direction with one or both hands (never with the fist).*

3. *A player cannot run with the ball. The player must throw it from the spot on which he catches it, allowance to be made for a man who catches the ball when running at a good speed if he tries to stop.*

4. *The ball must be held in or between the hands; the arms or body must not be used for holding it.*

5. *No shouldering, holding, pushing, tripping, or striking in any way the person of an opponent shall be allowed; the first infringement of this rule by any player shall count as a foul, the second shall disqualify him until the next goal is made, or, if there was evident intent to injure the person, for the whole of the game, no substitute allowed.*

6. *A foul is striking at the ball with the fist, violation of Rules 3, 4, and such as described in Rule 5.*

[†] The origin story of basketball, which once seemed ironclad—*Naismith and his peach baskets*—has been questioned in recent years. A photo has surfaced from the small town of Herkimer, New York, showing a group of young men holding what appears to be a basketball on which they've written "91–92," suggesting it was the season of 1891–92. The coach of this team, and also one of its players, Lambert Will, supposedly wrote a letter to James Naismith outlining the rules of what would come to be known as basketball. As the story goes in Herkimer: Naismith never responded; a few months later he introduced the game to his students with similar rules.

[*] Apparently Naismith asked the YMCA's janitor to bring him two boxes, which he planned to mount to the wall, but the man brought him two peach baskets instead. Instead of hunting down his intended shape, Naismith rolled with it, adapting on the fly, and calling his game "basket ball"—oh, how close we were to a sport called "box ball."

7. *If either side makes three consecutive fouls, it shall count a goal for the opponents (consecutive means without the opponents in the meantime making a foul).*

8. *A goal shall be made when the ball is thrown or batted from the grounds into the basket and stays there, providing those defending the goal do not touch or disturb the goal. If the ball rests on the edges, and the opponent moves the basket, it shall count as a goal.*

9. *When the ball goes out of bounds, it shall be thrown into the field of play by the person first touching it. In case of a dispute, the umpire shall throw it straight into the field. The thrower-in is allowed five seconds; if he holds it longer, it shall go to the opponent. If any side persists in delaying the game, the umpire shall call a foul on that side.*

origin of basketball -1891- SPRINGFIELD YMCA

MAKE A GOAL

13 RULES

a new game 1893

REFEREE KEEPS COUNT

15-MINUTE HALVES

10. *The umpire shall be judge of the men and shall note the fouls and notify the referee when three consecutive fouls have been made. He shall have power to disqualify men according to Rule 5.*

11. *The referee shall be judge of the ball and shall decide when the ball is in play, in bounds, to which side it belongs, and shall keep the time. He shall decide when a goal has been made, and keep account of the goals with any other duties that are usually performed by a referee.*

12. *The time shall be two fifteen-minute halves, with five minutes' rest between.*

13. *The side making the most goals in that time shall be declared the winner. In case of a draw, the game may, by agreement of the captains, be continued until another goal is made.*

It should be noted that the "ball," on this day, was actually a soccer ball, and looked nothing like a modern basketball, and actually more like something we'd today call a medicine ball, leathery and with stitches. As you've probably also already noted, the original rules made no room for what we today call *dribbling*. According to Naismith's notes, "When Mr. Stubbins brot [sic] up the peach baskets to the gym I secured them on the inside of the railing of the gallery. This was about 10 feet from the floor, one at each end of the gymnasium."⚹

A few months later, the Springfield College campus newspaper, *The Triangle*, was featuring articles about basket ball, headlined "A New Game," which was quickly growing in popularity. By 1893, the game was spreading across the country, as many of Naismith's pupils graduated with phys ed degrees and brought basket ball to their new jobs at various YMCAs in other states. And just five years later, the University of Kansas hired Naismith to start its men's college basketball program. (On that first Kansas team was a player named Forrest "Phog" Allen, who would go on to coach Dean Smith, who would go on to coach Michael Jordan.)

But most important—for our purposes—is the fact that just a few weeks after introducing the game of basket ball to his class at Springfield College, Naismith wrote about the game, and its rules, in the YMCA publication *Physical Education*.

Just a few miles down the road at Smith College, an all-women's school, a copy of the magazine crossed the desk of a woman named Senda Berenson. Which leads us into the next chapter of our story...

⚹ Seems as if the ten-foot height of the rim—er, the peach baskets—was not meticulously calculated by Naismith, but rather a choice of convenience: that's how high the gallery was above the gym floor. If it had been twelve feet between floor and gallery, perhaps the entire dimensions of the game would have been different.

SENDA
BERENSON

THE ORIGINAL HOOP MUSE

The woman who would come to be known as the "mother of women's basketball" also happened to be born in the country known as the Motherland...that is, Russia. In 1875, when she was seven years old, Senda Berenson emigrated from what is now Lithuania to the Boston area alongside her older brother. Ironically, Senda was a sickly child who valued music, books, and art above athletics. "Frail and delicate" were two words frequently used to describe her.

In her early twenties, Senda began exploring gymnastics to strengthen her physical condition and by 1892 found herself in charge of physical education at Smith College—an all-girls' school in Northampton, Massachusetts, that boasted some of the best facilities for women in the country. Two years after arriving at the college, Berenson wrote the following: "Until recent years, the so-called ideal woman was a small-waisted, small-footed, small-brained damsel, who prided herself on her delicate health, who thought fainting interesting, and hysterics fascinating."

Although Berenson thought that all young women should engage in physical activity, she also believed that activity shouldn't be too strenuous. This is why, upon reading about James Naismith's game of basket ball in a copy of the YMCA publication *Physical Education*, she slightly modified the rules to make it less cardiovascularly intense.[†] Berenson was unsure if her female students would enjoy the team game, as they'd only ever attempted solo activities.

But this new game of basket ball was so well received that the following year Berenson

[†] And, unlike Naismith's first game down the road, which used peach baskets, the first game played by women at Smith College used wastebaskets.

> ## ONE YOUNG WOMAN RESPONDED THAT 'BASKET BALL' HAD INCREASED HER 'ENDURANCE, LUNG CAPACITY, ALERTNESS, COURAGE, AND TOUGHNESS.'

arranged a scrimmage—played on March 22, 1893—between the freshman and sophomore classes. She also sought the feedback of her students, and one young woman responded that "basket ball" had increased her "endurance, lung capacity, alertness, courage, and toughness."

Berenson wanted to continue modifying the rules for her women, as she thought the sport was still too rough. She and her students decided to divide the court into three regions, and players were not allowed to leave their assigned region. In addition, players couldn't dribble more than three times, or hold the ball for more than three seconds, or grab the ball out of the opposition's hands.

Publications sought out Berenson—the first woman to discover the game—to edit the *Official Basket Ball Guide for Women*, beginning in 1901 and continuing for eighteen years. She was also the original chair of the United States Basket Ball Committee, which formed in 1905.

OCTOBER 1901

Spalding's Athletic Library

Basket Ball

for

Women

EDITED BY MISS SENDA BERENSON,
OF SMITH COLLEGE, NORTHAMPTON, MASS.

PUBLISHED BY THE
AMERICAN SPORTS PUBLISHING CO
16 and 18 Park Place, New York

February 26, 1892

Dear Diary,

It's been three weeks since my last entry and so much has happened. I can only say it was my good fortune to see a copy of PHYSICAL EDUCATION thrown away in the wastebasket under a fellow teacher's desk. Was it improper of me to fish it out? Certainly, it was unladylike. I heard one of the Russian literature teachers—the one who smiles kindly at me, unlike the others— use a phrase. He said, "The ends justify the means." Well, I must agree with him in this instance. (But I can't say yet if I will always agree with this new phrase. One must maintain their principles.)

This new game of basket ball excites me greatly. And the girls love it so. It's great fun to watch them sweat and run and compete. But I know I must not push the men too far, too fast. If we are to keep this game, I must compromise. I must make it softer and gentler, or it will be taken from us completely, I know. But, oh, the visions I have! I see a future of running and jumping. I see a future in which these young women make this game their own, as it surely must be.

For now, though, I can only share such thoughts here. We are in a tenuous place, we women, and I must not let great be the enemy of good. How I long to unleash these fine young women and let them play to their hearts' content! I can hear their joy and laughter ringing in my ears. But I know (oh, yes, how I know) that as quickly as basket ball has arrived at our door it can be taken away. The men already make noise about the time we take in the gym. They say it takes away from their physical pursuits, to which they feel more entitled. And I hear whispers of barring us completely.

This basket ball brings my young women too much joy to let this happen, so I will bend to their will so we do not break.

THE FIRST COLLEGIATE GAME

I magine people on the East Coast, clutching their pearls, terrified of letting women compete freely in this recently invented game of basket ball. *Too physical*, they claimed upon seeing women in action, *and immodest to boot!* But the rules of the game had already reached California, and the West Coast ladies didn't have such deep-rooted institutions (read: paternalism) calling the shots. (Though even in California, this would quickly change.)

The year was 1896, and women didn't yet have the right to vote, when nearly 700 spectators[1] —all women, as mixed crowds for such events were scandalous—gathered at the San Francisco Page Street Armory to watch Stanford University play the University of California. The game followed Senda Berenson's rules: the court was divided into thirds. This groundbreaking event drew interest from all of the big San Francisco newspapers, which sent women writers and artists to cover the action.[2] In the following weeks, news accounts of the landmark game even appeared in the *New York Times* and the *New York Sun*.

According to the *San Francisco Chronicle*, the armory was bumping with late-1800s enthusiasm, and the crowd "roared until the glass doors in the gun cases shivered at the noise." The same *Chronicle* writer noted that "there is not an instant of ennui[3] in basket ball. All is motion, change, excitement."

The game was tied 1–1 at the half[4] and ended with a 2–1 victory for Stanford. The game-winning bucket—a long toss from the shoulder[5]—was made by Stanford's Agnes Morley. The Stanford women were hailed upon their return to Palo Alto, even serenaded by the Stanford band.

But despite the sold-out crowd, and the nail-biting finish, and the wall-to-wall media coverage, the Stanford administration put an end to women's basket ball, and all women's team intercollegiate sports, just a few years later.

---

[1] The game was extremely popular among the women of Cal. Entry was fifty cents, and the accumulated profits were used by Cal to financially support the Cal men's track team and their upcoming East Coast tour. (So, yeah, at the beginning, women's sports subsidized the men!)

[2] Men, banned from the premises for reasons of modesty, nonetheless attempted to watch by climbing to the rooftop and peering in windows.

[3] Boredom.

[4] When the athletes snacked on orange slices.

[5] Inside the armory, neither hoop had backboards, and the women were only allowed to shoot single-handed.

According to the *Daily*, the campus newspaper, Stanford explained its 1899 decision as "for the good of the student's health" and that previous women's sports had drawn "unpleasant publicity"—and here the administration was almost certainly referring to this 1896 showdown between Stanford and Cal.

Even so, the women who made up the Stanford women's basket ball team traveled surreptitiously to Cal in 1900, crushed the Bears 7–0, then organized an independent club in Palo Alto. Before the crackdown on the early dawn of women's intercollegiate sports, the *New York Sun* described the inaugural showdown in the armory to its East Coast readers:

The new girl made her debut in the arena of intercollegiate sport in California last week, and opened up no end of entrancing possibilities for the future gaiety of nations, while putting up as pretty and smart an exhibition of athletics as has been seen on the Pacific slope. The women students of the University of California met the women students of Stanford University in a game of basketball in San Francisco for the championship of the coast. There have been games of basketball between girl teams before, but this was new in bringing together representative teams from two universities.

Stanford University helped start intercollegiate women's basketball. By the 1920s, though, only a small handful of four-year schools played intercollegiate women's games. The thinking went that the intense competition of a game distracted from the more genteel pursuit of simple exercise and good sportsmanship.

AUGUST 16, 1896

GIRLS PLAY BASKET BALL.

AND IN THIS CORNER

FORT SHAW, THE EARLIEST WORLD CHAMPIONS

When James Naismith invented the game of basketball in 1891, he did so in response to an edict from his boss: he had two weeks to devise an indoor game—and not too rowdy of one—that would keep students—well, boys, really—in shape during the long, harsh New England winters.

Actually, let's let Naismith tell the story himself—this is from a rare 1939 radio interview on the New York program *We the People*.

"One day I had an idea, I called the boys to the gym, divided them up into teams of nine and gave them a soccer ball," Naismith said. "I showed them two peach baskets I'd nailed up at each end of the gym, and I told them the idea was to throw the ball into the other team's peach basket...Ten years later basketball was being played all over the country...and the whole thing started with a couple of peach baskets I put up in a little gym forty-eight years ago. I guess it just goes to show what you can do if you have to."

It's that last sentence that's fascinating—*it just goes to show what you can do if you have to*. Naismith means it in the standard way: necessity being the mother of invention and all. But what strikes me is how applicable the line is to our story. Naismith was simply devising a game to keep his kids sane and fit during winter, but the by-product of his invention, when it soon landed in the hands of others was something even more rebellious and transgressive and...for brief moments, liberating.

This is the story of the Fort Shaw Indian Girls Basketball Team, who in 1904 were crowned world champions.

The ten girls who made up Fort Shaw's team: Rose LaRose, Flora Lucero, Katie Snell, Minnie Burton, Genevieve Healy, Sarah Mitchell, Emma Sansaver, Genie Butch, Belle Johnson, and Nettie Wirth.

Minnie was a great shooter, Belle was the versatile leader, Emma was the little playmaker, Nettie was a star with a prodigious leap, Gen was the impish one. Now it might seem obvious that sports, that a team, could provide solace, and a place to belong. But this concept—of finding out about yourself by playing sports with others—was an experience rarely offered to women back then.

"They came of age at a time when a fledgling game was being embraced by women and girls whose gender had thus far excluded them from participation in team sports," said Linda Peavy, whose book, with coauthor Ursula Smith, is *Full-Court Quest: The Girls from Fort Shaw Indian School, Basketball Champions of the World*.

But for the girls of Fort Shaw, it was an

FOR THE GIRLS ON FORT SHAW'S BASKETBALL TEAM, LIFE HAD NOT BEEN EASY.

experience that came with a price. In 1892, a fort that was located on Sun River in Montana, and on Blackfoot territory, became an Indian boarding school, where Indian kids were sent—often involuntarily—from tribes across Montana, Idaho, and Wyoming. It was, as Peavy explained, "an Indian boarding school that was supposed to strip them of all their old practices and teach them the white man's way."

Some kids who attended Fort Shaw hated it and ran away, others endured, and still others embraced—or at least saw the benefit of—learning English and the skills associated with what had become, at that point, the inevitable proliferation of the Western man's way of life. For the girls on Fort Shaw's basketball team, life had not been easy: four of them had already lost their mothers, two had lost their fathers, and while at school, two of their sisters would die from infectious disease.

"At that particular time, they were training the Indians to take their place among white or Indian society, but they were giving them English, they were giving them tools that made that possible," said Peavy.

And also around this same time, basketball—still two words—was spreading rapidly. But many young women never got a chance to play basketball with Naismith's rules, because the game had already been modified by female teachers to make it more "ladylike."

By sheer luck, or maybe it was destiny, the version of the game brought back to Fort Shaw by Josephine Langley in 1897—and the one played across much of the West—was Naismith's version. And even though the Native American culture traditionally encouraged the same enthusiasm for sports in girls as they did in boys, at Fort Shaw, basketball was the only sport the girls were allowed to participate in.

By 1902, when the school finished a new court, the girls of Fort Shaw—those ten girls I mentioned earlier—fell in love with the game. And they were really, really good. So good, in fact, that they would beat all comers and developed a reputation as the best team in the region.

This, from the PBS documentary *Playing for the World*, which aired in 2010: "The Fort Shaw team was now a huge attraction, winning games all across the state. On some trips they brought the school band with them for performances after the games. As the 1903 season continued, Coach Campbell scheduled games against college teams."

In that 1903 season, Fort Shaw defeated the University of Montana in front of 700 people, but they also faced racism and anti-Indian sentiment. They also struggled to find opponents. *Playing for the World* explains why, quoting the newspaper the *Anaconda Standard*. "Fort Shaw's famous girls basketball team has not been playing much throughout the state this season for the reason there is no girls team in the state who can give them anything like a tussle. They stand alone and unrivaled. This may not be pleasant reading for the white girls, but it is true."

But soon, an invitation came to play—to perform, really—at the 1904 World's Fair in St. Louis. The girls would live at the Model Indian School on the fairgrounds and demonstrate basketball, along with other skills—sewing, music—they'd learned at school. The world's fair of 1904 was to celebrate the Louisiana Purchase.

(Quick history lesson: the Louisiana Purchase was when the United States bought 828,000 square miles of land from Napoleon's France for $15 million in 1803, the swath of land stretching from Montana, down at a slight angle through what is now Denver, and all the way to New Orleans.)

"The thrust of this fair had been to show the path of progress, once you opened up the west," Peavy said. "If you think about it in American history was all about progress, progress, progress—like electricity, too—and they were all on display, but then they had the Indians also on display because, after all, they were what we were leaving behind."

The team focused on the opportunity the fair presented them, more than the oddity of being gawked at, and more than anything they reveled in their skill, and teamwork, on the court—a fast-paced style of play that no other team could match.

Here is a description of the final game at the 1904 World's Fair, when the Fort Shaw girls played the all-white Missouri All-Stars. This, from the opening pages of *Full-Court Quest*:

Inside the model Indian school itself, the girls from Fort Shaw were donning navy middies and bloomers then helping one another add the final touch: a bright little ribbon of silk at the end of each girl's long braid. Their shoes were tightly laced, their stockings pulled up and bound so not a wrinkle showed between shoe tops and bloomer hems.

AT FORT SHAW, BASKETBALL WAS THE ONLY SPORT THE GIRLS WERE ALLOWED TO PARTICIPATE IN.

With their appearance a roar went up through the crowd...and the cheers continued as someone bounced the ball on the concrete floor of the porch. A quick pass around, a few dribbles, then the entire team fell into place, all 10 of them, two lines of five, standing as if in military formation, for the intra-mural train had pulled into Indian Station and the Missouri All-Stars were stepping off the train and onto the platform—suited up and ready for the game that would determine the champions of the 1904 St. Louis World's Fair.

In the months after beating everyone at the world's fair, the team made public their desire for games, for better competition. This from an article in the *Great Falls Tribune* under the headline, "THEY CHALLENGE THE WHOLE WORLD: Fort Shaw Basketball Girls Willing to Play Against Any Girls Team in Existence":

"Billy Adams, physical instructor of the Fort Shaw Indian school and coach of the crack girls basketball team…is probably one of the happiest men in the city, and deservedly so, for his team of Indian maidens have yet to meet its equal on the basketball floor."

But the young women of Fort Shaw would never quite get the chance to grow with the game. The school closed just a few years later. And in many parts of the country, specifically at universities, faculty banned female students from competitive play. The shining wonder that was Fort Shaw faded from memory and has been almost entirely buried by history. But what hasn't been lost, and could never be, is the ripple effect this long-ago team had: Fort Shaw is just one reason for the indelible connection between Native Americans and basketball.

"Naismith wanted a game that would give his boys activity within the confines of a New England winter, but what people liked was football," Peavy said. "They really wanted boys to be tough. Indian boys played football, too… and I think Fort Shaw did have an impact there because it became known earlier on, that these Indian girls, every place you went, you wanted to have baskets up, you wanted to start your players and it doesn't take a lot of equipment to play basketball."

And there was something else, too; a through-line connecting those ten girls from 1904 to today.

"For many, many young people now, playing basketball is your only chance for college or your only chance to get out of whatever place you're stuck in," Peavy said. "And I think part of the reason their teamwork developed so well was out of the sense that this was their ticket to doing something that nobody could do better."

JACKLYN JONES

These young girls held the game so close to them.

Yea, it meant the world to them it seems.

It was a glimpse of something new.

RULES, RULES, RULES

THE MAKING OF THE GAME

The early days of basketball are confusing. Today, in order to change even the smallest rule, a committee is convened, and a vote is taken. But back in the beginning, individuals were deciding how this newly invented game should be played. And sometimes the perspective of that single person, from so long ago, makes little sense to us now. Because back then, and especially for women, the rules of the game were not determined so much by what made the game better, or more exciting, or more fun, but rather what was more…ladylike. And back then, sweating and contact and joy—these things were very unladylike.

And that is how we end up with a smorgasbord of early rules for the game, which at the time was still two words: basket ball. On the East Coast, most women played with Senda Berenson's rules. The court was divided into thirds to limit running and contact, and you couldn't hold the ball for more than three seconds or dribble more than three times. Kind of lame.

But across the country, out in the West, many women's teams played by men's rules. (Perhaps these were the first to reach the coast.) And in the South, most women were playing with Clara Gregory Baer's rules. She was a teacher in New Orleans, at Sophie Newcomb College. In 1895, she staged a game of "basquette" in front of an all-female audience of 560 people at the Southern Athletic Club. Following Baer's rules, the court was divided into as many sections as players per side, and you couldn't dribble or guard anyone, or shoot with two hands, and you could only run when the ball was in the air, and then only inside your designated area. Kind of weird.

So, across the country, women were playing either with Berenson Rules, or Baer Rules, or, occasionally, with men's rules. It's hard to even visualize how the game was being played, and many of these iterations were very different from the game we know today. Back then, depending on where you were in the country,

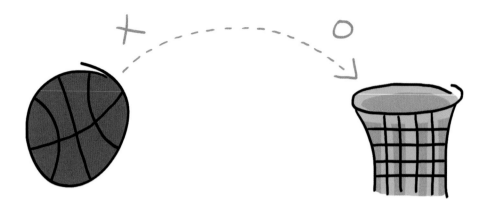

dribbling was either allowed or not—and the same for using a backboard, or guarding people, or stealing the ball, and so on. For the 1910–1911 season, according to the NCAA, "dribbling is eliminated," only to have it return—with a maximum of just one dribble allowed!—a year later. Kind of confusing.

Perhaps the only common overlap in all these versions of the game was the main objective: putting a ball-like object into a basket-like goal.

To understand the politics and social pressure at play, it helps to read some news clippings from the first few years of the game. Here's this from the November 17, 1895, edition of the *New York Times*:

"Girls football," as the popular basket ball is called by patronizing college students of the stronger sex, is, although shorn of some of the rougher features that make the former a menace to life and limb, not precisely a drawing-room performance. It is usually played in colleges for women between the juniors and sophomores in the gymnasium and in gymnasium dress. There are intense excitement, shrill feminine screams and hurrahs, waving of class banners, and encouragement of favorite players. The agility and strength displayed at a recent contest were remarkable and spoke highly for the development of the new woman.

But then there is this from a few years later—the December 16, 1899, edition of the *San Francisco Call*:

Faculty at Stanford Abolishes Basket-ball. Considers That the Game Is Too Severe a Physical Strain on the Young Women.

The faculty athletic committee at a meeting held last night passed a ruling virtually abolishing the game of basket-ball when played by young ladies of the university. The rule forbids any intercollegiate contest between the young women which requires team work, and further provides that all contests must be played on the home campus. It is not intended that the game of tennis should come within this rule. The reasons given by the faculty athletic committee for placing such restrictions upon women's athletics is that the physical strain upon the young women is too great.

The 1900s steadily marched forward, but "progress" was not linear for our beloved game. Eventually, beginning in the late 1910s and into the early 1920s, the country became more unified in its approach, but parts of the country—for example, in Iowa and Oklahoma—played six-on-six, which limited girls to only playing in one half of the court, until as late as the mid-nineties.

All of these iterations, and fits and starts, eventually lead us to the present: the game we now know, in all its physical complexity. Which is kind of cool.

Basquette

BY CLARA GREGORY BAER

New Orleans CIRCA 1895

"IN ONE OF THE FASTEST GAMES OF THE SEASON. . ." STARRING

ISADORE "IZZY" CHANNELS

Solomon "Sol" Butler was one of the greatest multisport athletes of his era, representing the United States in the long jump in the 1920 Olympics, signing with the National Football League in 1923, and playing baseball briefly for the Kansas City Monarchs in the Negro leagues. In 1925, Butler even quarterbacked alongside the legendary Jim Thorpe for the Canton Bulldogs.

But our interest in Butler runs parallel to his playing career. In the 1920s, the sports star became immersed in Chicago's amateur athletic scene, and in 1921 he formed the Roamer Athletic Club, known as Roamer A.C., and eventually the Roamer Girls—an African American women's club basketball team that was considered the best Black team in the country throughout the early 1920s.

According to the Black Fives Foundation, which works to preserve the history of African American basketball, the squad debuted on

March 19, 1921, at the 8th Regiment Armory on Chicago's South Side. The small write-up in the local paper read, "In one of the fastest games of the season and the first of its kind, the girls put themselves on record when the Roamer A.C. of Grace Presbyterian Sunday school, coached by 'Sol' Butler, defeated the Cosmopolitans of the Olivet Sunday school to the score of 26 to 22."

The star of the Roamers was Isadore "Izzy" Channels, who was also a tennis champion and considered one of the greatest female athletes of her era. One of the leading Black papers, the *Chicago Defender*, wrote about Channels in 1925: "Scoring and passing at will and even at times joking, she played a game far above the heads of her opponents and far in advance of her colleagues."

The Roamers played both Black and white teams (like the Harvey Bloomers and Taylor Trunks), drawing crowds for its style of play.

Attending a Roamers A.C. game was often a social event in Chicago. Then, toward the end of the decade, Izzy Channels retired, and some of the Roamers' biggest stars—Corinne Robinson and Virginia Willis—left the team to join the Savoy Colts.

As the Roamers faded away, the Colts came to prominence with another generational star, Ora Washington. At first, the two-sport star (like Channels, she was also a tennis champ) spent her winters playing for the Colts in Chicago, but by the early 1930s Washington helped anchor another legendary club team, the Philadelphia Tribunes.

The Savoy Colts were eventually replaced by a team that would travel the country: the Club Store Co-Eds, aka the Chocolate Co-Eds, who became a traveling mainstay for the next twenty years.

CHICAGO,
CHICAGO, CHICAGO
AND THE

CLUB STORE
CO-EDS

⚡

The 1935 advertisement read, "Super Attraction Basketball! World's Champion Colored Girls' Basketball Team. Featuring the Tallest Girl in the World—Helen 'Streamline' Smith, 7 feet tall. This will be a novelty that you should see."

The team being advertised, starring Helen Smith, was a local Chicago squad called the Club Store Co-Eds. The team took its name from its sponsor, the Club Store, which was located on Black Chicago's main business street. In the decades before World War II, the game of basketball was thriving in the Midwest, especially Chicago. One of the predecessors to the famed Harlem Globetrotters was a club called the Savoy Big Five, a men's team promoted by Dick Hudson, who then turned his attention to the women's game.

The Club Store Co-Eds were organized by Hudson in November 1934. Quickly, the team became the best in Chicago, with a lineup featuring Smith, Zadie Lloyd, Katie Bard, and sisters Ruth and Sara Reese. Just like its Chicago predecessor, Roamer A.C., the Co-Eds were beating everyone in the city. After a year of just playing in Chicago, Dick Hudson decided

to take the Co-Eds on the road, and by January 1935, the team was touring the heartland of America as a "novelty" act, playing boys' and men's teams. And just like the Roamers before them, the Co-Eds recruited a tennis star to its roster, Lulu Porter, the national ATA grass court champion.

The Co-Eds hit small towns across America for many years, and Hudson was ahead of his time in exaggerating the heights of his players. Smith, for example, was nowhere near seven feet tall; she was, according to most records of the day, actually six foot four, but that didn't stop local journalists from hyping up the Co-Eds with lines reminiscent of the Globetrotters—*The Greatest Show in the World!*

Over the years, the club recruited star talent, including two-time Olympian runner Tidye Pickett, the first African American woman to compete in the Olympic games, and who also happened to be one of the best players in the Negro church leagues before joining the Co-Eds. Selling a traveling show, year after year—and before the advent of television—relied on a lot of marketing gimmicks, and like many Black athletes and performers, the Co-Eds eventually adopted a name that identified them by race, promoting themselves as the Chocolate Co-Eds.

Here's how the *History of Sport* summarizes the juxtaposition of making a living as a women's basketball player in the 1930s and 1940s, while also being positioned as a sideshow. "This glimpse into the world of barnstorming in the early 1940s that the Chocolate Co-Eds were experiencing reveals that it could be a degrading experience," wrote Robert Pruter. "To draw gullible small town crowds to the contests, the team was presented almost as freaks (their race was made a part of their beyond-normal description) with P. T. Barnum–type exaggeration of their achievements, athletic abilities, and physiques. One wonders, for example, what Tidye Pickett thought as she played under the name Chocolate Co-Eds, gave a demonstration of her sprinting ability on a basketball court, and being described as the 'fastest girl runner in the world.' Was it pride of getting recognition for her athletic ability, or a bit of humiliation at being put on display like a circus sideshow act?"

The last season for the Club Store Co-Eds was 1950. Why? Well, televisions began appearing in the homes of an increasing number of Americans, leaving them less need for local entertainment options. Still, the legacy of early teams like the Co-Eds is complex—they faced issues with regard to race, gender, exploitation—but their existence reinforces one foundational truth: across time and geography and race, women have always longed to play, in whatever context available to them.

THRILLING BASKETBALL...
RATED FAMILY
ENTERTAINMENT...
CLEVER...BRILLIANT...
POWERFUL ACTION

THE BARNSTORMING RED HEADS

The All-American Red Heads were founded in 1936, just ten years after the Harlem Globetrotters, and the two teams have plenty in common: both are (or, in the case of the Red Heads, *were*) a touring troupe of hoopers, whose games included trick shots and jokes; both existed more to entertain crowds than as cutthroat competitors; and both always won way more games than they lost.

But that's where the similarity ends. The All-American Red Heads were all women (and, yes, all redheaded...thanks to hair dye!), and the team was never racially integrated. The team was founded in Missouri during Jim Crow, and the All-American Red Heads played as many as 200 games a year for more than five decades... without ever suiting up a Black player.

Still, the team broke plenty of other barriers and remains the longest-running women's professional team in history. The team's founders, Mr. and Mrs. C. M. Olson, first owned a male exhibition team called Olson's Terrible Swedes. Mrs. Olson ran a beauty salon, and the antics of the "Terrible Swedes" inspired Mrs. Olson and the women who worked in her shops. After work, many of the women liked to shoot baskets at a nearby hoop. Two of the women were natural redheads. Believing he needed a gimmick to promote a women's team, Mr. Olson had the non-redheaded women use henna, a natural dye. And that's how the All-American Red Heads were born.

In the early years, the team played mostly in rural America, against local men's teams. They would often draw a crowd of 2,000 people in towns that only had a population of 3,000. The team once won ninety-six games in ninety-six days, and in 1940 became the first professional basketball team to play in the Philippines—drawing a crowd of 10,000.

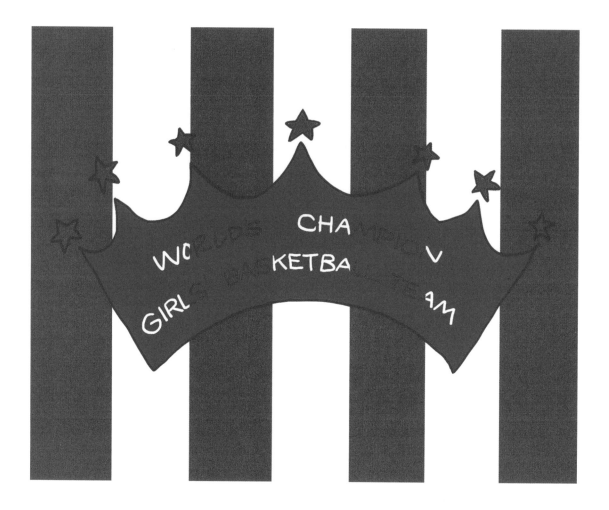

The Red Heads often leaned into the sexism and stigma of the day, trading on the novelty of watching women in athletic competition. One promotional piece used by the team itself read: "The woman's place is in the home was the battle cry of 19th Century American gentlemen. What a triumph for the weaker sex when the dream of equal suffrage became stark, startling reality. Now wouldn't you think these women would be satisfied with their age-old rule of the man at home and a half interest in the ballot box? Not the All-American Red Heads!"

In 1974, *Sports Illustrated* published the article, "ALL RED, SO HELP THEM HENNA, with a subtitle that read, "To make this team a girl has to dye her hair, but she also has to be a first-rate athlete. Then she can play 200 nights a year, humiliating out-of-shape men." The article began with this line: "This is the best women's basketball team in North America. That can be said unequivocally, and you do not even know their names."

In those later years, the team's star was a lanky lefty named Karen Logan. She wanted to regain her amateur status to try out for the US women's basketball team in 1976, which was the inaugural year for the women's game as an Olympic sport. "I'd give anything to play the Chinese team or the Russians," Logan told *Sports Illustrated*. "I'd love to have a chance at the AAU champions or any women's team anywhere. We could beat anyone in the world. I'm sure of it. But we'll never know. No one will ever know because we never play anyone but has-been men."

 WE COULD BEAT ANYONE IN THE WORLD. I'M SURE OF IT. BUT WE'LL NEVER KNOW.
—KAREN LOGAN

THE MIGHTY MACS

A MIRACULOUS DYNASTY

the Mighty Macs
a miraculous dynasty

ometimes, a handful of talented players all grow up in the same area, at the same time, and something inexplicable—something a little like fate—brings them together onto the same court.

There is no other explanation, other than destiny, for what happened at little Immaculata College in the 1970s. No grand scheme existed to turn this tiny all-girls' college, just a short drive from Philadelphia, into a basketball powerhouse.

What happened was simple: a number of young women in the city had grown up playing the game, and they'd come to Immaculata to study—it was a place with a reputation for creating opportunities for young women—at the same moment a fiery young coach was also stepping on campus.

The school was founded in 1920; its teachers were nuns and priests, and like many schools across the country, Immaculata encouraged its female students to play basketball. But not in any serious, ultra-competitive way. At least, not until Cathy Rush arrived.

Rush was twenty-two years old. She was married to an NBA referee. And in 1970, she accepted an offer of $450 a year to coach Immaculata's women's basketball team. As the legend goes, after the first day of practice, Rush came home and told her husband: "I have some players."

And she did. Most notably, a six-foot post player named Theresa Shank, who would go on to anchor the Mighty Macs' unprecedented run: the first three national titles under the Association for Intercollegiate Athletics for Women (AIAW) umbrella, which governed women's basketball until the NCAA took over in the early eighties.

To understand the Mighty Macs, a few illuminating details: For their first three seasons under Rush, the Immaculata uniform was

1975 12,000 SPECTATORS WATCH IMMACULATA

a blue wool tunic; the next two seasons the players wore skirts; and only in 1976 did the team finally evolve to wearing shorts. All along the way, the girls would buy and wear their own white Converse Chuck Taylors—the staple shoe of hoopers everywhere. "We were moving out of the days of 'young ladies shouldn't sweat; women shouldn't be involved in sports,' to 'hey, this is not only OK, it's healthy; it's a good thing; it can give you confidence and all of the great benefits and intangibles that come with playing team sports,'" Marianne Stanley, another of the team's stars, told ESPN back in 2008. "The change in the uniforms is symbolic of all that change."

As Immaculata was turning into a powerhouse, in 1972, a little piece of legislation called Title IX was passed in Congress that, ironically, and unbeknownst to them, would ensure that Immaculata's run would be short-lived.

But before colleges everywhere began (per law) funneling money into their women's programs, Immaculata was the best team in the country—and everyone on the small campus knew it.

Back then, when you walked into Camilla Hall, where the team played, the first three rows would be filled with nuns in full garb. And, of course, they would pray...for an Immaculata victory.

"I think there was a mystique and a power that was unmistakable, that people recognized," Stanley told ESPN. "They may have not understood what it was, but they knew there was something at work greater than everybody, and it was on our side. That's a heck of a sixth man."

In the years after Immaculata's run in the seventies, which ended with Rush's retirement in 1977, many of the Mighty Macs went on to coach: Grentz (née Shank) became the first full-time head coach in the country, at Rutgers; Stanley coached at Old Dominion, and Rene Portland at Penn State.

"To look at the circumstances of Theresa, Marianne Stanley, Rene Portland, all the other wonderful players, myself, all to arrive at this place at that time, you have to think there was some divine intervention," Rush told ESPN. "And all of us believed that the faith that these nuns had in us, and the power of prayer helped us do everything we did."

THE REVOLUTION BEGINS...
OFF THE FIELD

TITLE IX

⚡

The modern revolution of women in sports was jump-started by something small: a rejection letter from the University of Virginia.

Former Indiana senator Birch Bayh told this story in a speech he gave in 2007: "My wife, Marvella Hern Bayh, was probably the most important thing that had ever happened in my life. When we had started talking over lunch, it was clear that both of us wanted to make a difference with our lives, but we weren't quite sure what...Her dream was to be admitted to the University of Virginia. Her request was returned, 'Women need not apply.' This was the first time she had been told she could not do something, not because she was not qualified, but because she happened to be a young woman."

More than a decade later, Bayh, along with congresswomen Edith Green and Patsy Mink, helped spearhead the passage of Title IX, which was part of the Education Amendments of 1972.

Oddly enough, the words that would forever change sports did not actually include the word "sports" or even refer to them at all. And yet, the piece of legislation signed into law by Richard Nixon in 1972—that is, Title IX—opened the (gym) door for millions of young girls, who came pouring inside, ready to play. Title IX is technically an education bill, meant to level the academic playing field. The fact that its impact has been felt most acutely in sports—well, that's been a surprise even to the authors of the bill. "We had no idea," Bernice Sandler, who helped write Title IX, told ESPN. "We had no idea how bad the situation really was—we didn't even use the word sex discrimination back then—and we certainly had no sense of the revolution we were about to start."

Here is the paragraph that would change everything: "No person in the United States shall, on the basis of sex, be excluded from participation in, be denied the benefits of, or be subjected to discrimination under any educational program or activity receiving Federal financial assistance."

Oh, the transformation this sparked! In the forty years after Title IX became law, girls playing high school sports increased more than tenfold; girls playing college sports more than sixfold. The premise of Title IX was simple: whatever existed in school for boys must also

"No person in the United States shall, on the basis of sex, be excluded from participation in, be denied the benefits of, or be subjected to discrimination under any educational program or activity receiving Federal financial assistance."

THE CHANGE THAT CAME FROM THESE 37 WORDS CANNOT BE OVERSTATED

exist for girls. (Not that schools always lived up—or *live* up—to this ideal, but that's what's codified into law.)

The change that came from these thirty-seven words cannot be overstated.

Before 1972, the options for young girls were limited. Not much was available to them beyond the "tomboy" (*eye roll*) years of running around the neighborhood playing capture the flag or pickup sports. Whereas boys had Little League and pee wee football and CYO basketball, girls had, in some states, almost nothing. Sure, an industrious little girl could play on the boys' team for a few years, but by the time middle school rolled around, that was frowned upon. And playing sports in high school? In many places that was possible, yes, but it was often social suicide. So girls who longed for teamwork and athletic competition often became cheerleaders, where they could get a dose of those things—even if they could only be attained while rooting on the boys.

But then Title IX happened and, slowly but surely, the young girls started walking through the open doors. And as the years passed and the 1970s became the 1980s, the dynamic about what was cool for girls started shifting, too, until pretty soon, by the 1990s, girls playing sports wasn't a rarity—an anomaly—but rather the default.

And what sport did millions of young girls flock toward?

That's right—basketball.

A CASE STUDY
Remember Stanford University?

Let's check back in with the Stanford Cardinal, the squad who played the first women's intercollegiate game in 1896. The university banned the sport—remember they called it *unladylike*—but by 1974 the school was again officially sponsoring a women's basketball team. Title IX had just passed. But no watch group existed, ensuring that colleges were following the law. Perhaps unsurprisingly, most athletic departments tried to ignore Title IX, just crossed their fingers and hoped nobody complained.

A full two years after Title IX passed, the Stanford team was still playing in a gym that could barely hold a few dozen people. They were coached by a graduate student, wore cotton t-shirts as jerseys, and taped their own ankles. Mariah Burton Nelson played for Stanford at the time ⚡ and went on to write the groundbreaking book *The Stronger Women Get, the More Men Love Football.* She and her teammates soon realized that nobody was coming to help them. If they wanted better treatment, more funding, they would have to fight for it. They began showing up unannounced at the office of athletic director Dick DiBiaso.

⚡ *Burton Nelson also played for the New Jersey Gems of the Women's Professional Basketball League.*

"We just showed up without an appointment, sat in the lobby until he agreed to see us, then listed our complaints, demands, and requests," Burton Nelson told the authors of *Shattering the Glass*, Pamela Grundy and Susan Shackelford. "We got increasingly persistent. We told him Title IX had passed and that it was his job to start implementing it, that it was unfair to discriminate."

Burton Nelson estimated the players met with DiBiaso more than two dozen times in two years. Their fight yielded results. By 1976, the team had two full-time coaches, a trainer, and real uniforms. Plus, they had moved out of their tiny little gym into Maples Pavilion, where the Cardinal still play today. In 1978, the school would award their first scholarships for women's basketball.

Today, Stanford is one of the most legendary programs in women's basketball history—and with a long, and twisting, history of its own.

PAT SUMMITT

THE STEELY GAZE DEBUTS AT TENNESSEE

We can't know when Pat Summitt's famous glare was first deployed, or on whom, but we do know when Coach Summitt, one of the game's most important figures—and perhaps its *most* important— first arrived on the campus that she would forever change.

The year was 1974, and folks were belting out Barbra Streisand's "The Way We Were" (although the folks in Tennessee were probably also listening to Elvis and a little Dolly Parton), movie theaters were jammed with people seeing *Blazing Saddles*, and Patricia Sue Head was twenty-two years old as she started work at the University of Tennessee in Knoxville as teacher and graduate assistant for the basketball team. Perhaps her sharp look was perfected on a brother or sister—she was the fourth of five kids raised on a Tennessee farm—but she attributed its origin to her dad.

"I guess I got that from my father," Summitt once told NPR. "He was a man that was very focused and driven. And I grew up on a dairy farm. So, you know, cows never— they don't take a day off on a dairy farm. So, we milked at five a.m. and five p.m., and he just really, he demanded a lot from the five children, but in a good way. I don't think I would have this work ethic or this drive, or probably the stare. But with that, I think that just represents my focus and my intensity."

The look, it did not come with words. All the information, Pat Summitt figured, was already inside the person who the look was directed at. The stare was more of a prompt: *dig deeper, you know precisely why I'm not happy.* Debby Jennings, the longtime sports information director for Summitt's Lady Vols, said, "We all got that steely gaze, but there was always intent behind it; she didn't just throw it out there. It came with a message, and we were expected to know, in that moment, what the message was."

In those first years as coach, Summitt was really just a kid herself. Within months of starting the job as graduate assistant, the head coach abruptly quit, and Summitt was thrust into the top role. Plus, she was still playing the game herself. She'd played four years at the University of Tennessee–Martin, graduating the same year she took the job in Knoxville, then two years later she won a silver medal at the 1976 Summer Olympics in Montreal— the first time women's basketball was played.

Pat Summitt came from a world, and an era, where you scrapped and clawed for every little thing, including players' tenuous grip on access to athletics. In those early years at Tennessee, little was taken care of that Summitt didn't do herself. She taught classes—"The Coaching of Basketball with Pat Summitt," for aspiring coaches—and took the post seriously, failing anyone who didn't match her dedication. And when it came to her Lady Vols, she raised money for uniforms by selling doughnuts and she famously drove the team's white van.

"One time, for a road game, we actually slept in the other team's gym the night before," she told *TIME* magazine. "We had mats, we had our little sleeping bags. When I was a player, we played at Tennessee Tech for three straight games, and we didn't wash our uniforms. We only had one set. We played because we loved the game. We didn't think anything about it."

The legendary glare for which Summitt became known seemed to spring from her deep love of the game, keen understanding of the stakes for women, and strict childhood on the farm. Game after game, year after year, the future Hall of Fame coach shepherded the young women under her guidance, using a mixture of love, wisdom, home cooking, and that iron gaze that implored them to find more, find better.

"That look would be, 'What are you doing, get yourself in the game!'" said Semeka Randall, who won the 1998 NCAA title playing for Summitt, the team going 39–0. "That look meant everything. If you're locked into her, you knew what she expected of you. You knew Pat's heart; you knew that was her focused look. It's *go-time, baby*, and we need to make sure she doesn't have to repeat anything to us."

The stories of Pat Head Summitt are many—you'll read more later in this book— but they all began in 1974, when she won her first of 1,098 games, when she first squinted those crystal blue eyes, locked eyes with a young player, and inspired them to something greater.

★ Although Pat believed in hard work and was the "salt of the earth," she was also superstitious and would pick up (and look for) heads-up pennies before every game. Everyone around her knew this and would be on the lookout for pennies at arenas and before and after team shootarounds.

★ She was born in 1952 in Clarksville, Tennessee.

★ During her first season at UT, four of her players were only *one year* younger than she was.

★ In 1984 she was the head coach of Team USA at the Los Angeles Olympics, where the women won their first Olympic gold medal. (USSR boycotted the event.)

MARGARET AND LUSIA

DELTA STATE DOMINATES THE SEVENTIES

They burned their uniforms in response. Back in the 1930s, the game could be ripped out from under players. Out of nowhere, a university's board would issue an edict: no more basketball for women; the game is too strenuous. This was the heartbreaking circumstance in which Margaret Wade, star of the Delta State University team, and her teammates found themselves in 1932. In her first three collegiate seasons, Wade's squad had gone 28–5–2, then before her senior season, the administration released a statement: "Intercollegiate basketball could not be defended on sound grounds."

"THE FIRST TRULY DOMINANT PLAYER"

Pat Summitt knew Lucy Harris intimately; the two were teammates on the 1976 US Olympic team, which took the silver medal in Montreal, the first time that women's basketball was included in the Olympic Games. Harris actually scored the first points in Olympic history—not just for Team USA, but for the sport—with a bucket against Japan in the opening game.

That next year, the New Orleans Jazz launched Harris into the national headlines when the team selected her in the seventh round of the 1977 NBA Draft. She was taken ahead of thirty-three men. This move by the Jazz made Harris the first woman officially drafted into the NBA. (In 1969, the San Francisco Warriors drafted Denise Long, but the league office voided the pick.)

Harris declined to attend the Jazz training camp that year. She told the media that she knew she was a dominant force on the court, "but with the men, well, that's something different." Two years later, she returned to the court and played a season with the Houston Angels of the Women's Professional Basketball League (WBL), but mostly she focused on her family and education, letting the game become a thing of her past.

Here, let's let her coach, Margaret Wade, have the final word on her star player. "Lucy was mean underneath the boards," Wade told the *Clarion-Ledger*. "When she wanted to score, she could score. But the thing I liked about Lucy was, she was a team player. She did what the team needed, and that's why we were successful."

Too tough for young ladies, they said. What could Wade and her teammates do? Not a thing. "So," she said, "we burned our uniforms."

This is a foundational piece of Wade's story, of how her life eventually came full circle. Because forty-one years later—in 1973—Delta State finally reinstated its women's basketball program. (Thank you, Title IX.) And who did Delta State want at the helm? You guessed it. The school hired Wade as its head coach. That same year, a freshman named Lusia "Lucy" Harris enrolled on campus. Nearly a half century after that soul-crushing decision, the basketball gods had smiled on Margaret Wade. What happened next would forever change women's basketball.

Lucy Harris was six foot three and 185 pounds of muscle. She'd learned the game playing in her family's backyard in Mississippi, against her brothers, and she'd molded her game to be defensive and blend well with others. She had strong footwork on the block, a soft touch, and explosiveness toward the rim. In her book *Sum It Up*, Pat Summitt called Harris "the first truly dominant player of modern women's basketball." It's trite, but true: Lucy Harris was ahead of her time.

That first season with the combo punch of Wade and Harris—alongside fellow freshman Wanda Hairston—Delta State went 16–2, but failed to advance to the AIAW national tournament. (The AIAW ran a sixteen-team national

championship tournament for basketball from 1972 to 1982, after which the NCAA took over.)

But that next season, something special started to happen. Wade recruited a trio of players to join Harris and Hairston: guard Debbie Brock, Ramona Von Boeckman, and Cornelia Ward. Speaking of those five players, Wade told sportswriter Lee Baker: "They were a special team. They had a mutual admiration. They were smart, talented and wanted to win. They did not know how to lose…A mediocre girls' team will accept defeat. Those five never would."

Starting three freshmen and two sophomores, Delta State went undefeated all season, advancing to the AIAW national tournament, where they ran into juggernaut Immaculata College, winners of three consecutive titles. In that title game, Harris scored thirty-two points and grabbed sixteen rebounds as the Statesmen beat Immaculata for the national title. The game, for the first time ever, was played on national television.

Across that season and the next, Delta State won fifty-one consecutive games. When Harris finished her collegiate career, in 1977, she did so by winning her third straight national championship. In their four years together—and the first four of the rebooted Delta State program—Wade and Harris went 109–5.

In the *New York Times* Oscar-winning

documentary about Harris, *The Queen of Basketball*, she looked slyly at the camera and said: "The men's team didn't sell out as well as the women's team. We began to travel on airplanes. As a matter of fact, the men didn't fly. I guess the women were bringing in the money."

The team's sports information director, Langston Rogers, told *Mississippi Today*, "It was the greatest time of my professional life. That was such a great basketball team and took me to places, like Madison Square Garden, I had never dreamed of going. My gosh, what a team."

★ Delta State is in Mississippi.

★ The top collegiate player is awarded the Wade Trophy, which is named for Lily Margaret Wade; the first to win was Carol Blazejowski of Montclair State.

★ In the 1976–77 season, Delta State played Immaculata and Montclair State played Queens College in a doubleheader at Madison Square Garden in front of 12,336 fans.

★ Margaret Wade was one of the first three women—along with Senda Berenson Abbott and Bertha Teague—inducted into the Naismith Hall of Fame in 1986.

BASKETBALL LORE

"SUMMITT TWO TANKS"

Before the charter buses and the catered meals that the Lady Vols of Tennessee came to enjoy, there were the early days when nobody did just one job—they couldn't afford to.

Pat Summitt wasn't just the head coach. She also washed the uniforms and drove the team van. Back in those days, the late seventies, the team had a sixteen-seat white Ford van with the orange UT crest on the doors. They also had a station wagon. Pat drove the van. And she did so like she did most everything: fast.

The players piled into the van, and either an assistant coach or Debby Jennings, the media director, drove the station wagon. This arrangement happened a thousand times over the years, but one trip in particular stands out.

It was the week before Christmas, 1978, and Tennessee traveled to Mississippi University for Women, in Columbus, for the school's annual holiday tournament. The Lady Vols were the favorite. They should have won. Alas, they did not—a fact that left Coach Summitt irate. "Seems we were already home from Christmas!" she yelled at her squad.

The next morning, a few lucky players went home with their parents. The rest piled into the van, with Summitt behind the wheel and not a word being spoken. Debby and the rest of the crew followed behind, noting that nobody in the vehicle ahead of them seemed to be talking, or, really, even moving. Faces forward, still. She also noticed they hadn't stopped for breakfast, and it was a six-hour drive back to Knoxville.

OK, all right, that's cool, she thought. Because at some point they'd need to stop for gas. A little while later she picked up the CB radio that connected the two vehicles and she said, "Hey, Pat, this is DJ, we're under a quarter of a tank, close to an eighth, and we were wondering if we were stopping for gas soon." She pulled out the gas card and added: "Looks like there's a Shell or a Pilot soon."

After a beat Pat responded: "Mmm-hmm."

"So are you low on gas?" Debby asked. "I need to get gas."

"I'll get back to you," said Pat.

They kept driving, the tank kept emptying, the needle kept dipping. Debby's concern kept rising. Finally, Pat's voice crackled across the radio: "What's your gas situation?"

Debby fired back: "Almost dead—on E."

"Reach to the left side underneath the wheel and pull out the lever."

Debby reached beneath and found the handle Pat had described.

"Now flip it over," Pat said.

Confused, Debby did as the head coach had said, then stared as the needle slowly started to rise—the tank was filling up.

"Dual gas tanks," said Pat, then signed off. The van didn't stop until early afternoon, until it was parked in the UT campus lot.

The night before, Summitt had taken the van, then the wagon, and filled up both tanks—hell-bent on making her point. What point, you might ask? That's up for interpretation, but it's one of many stories that make up the Pat Summitt lore.

PAT SUMMITT WASN'T JUST THE HEAD COACH. SHE ALSO WASHED THE UNIFORMS AND DROVE THE TEAM VAN.

THE DREAM BEGINS

A LEGENDARY VERSION OF TEAM USA STEPS ONTO THE STAGE

When the women's game debuted at the Olympics in Montreal, in 1976, the only other team on anyone's radar was the Soviet Union. The Russian squad was dominant. Uljana Semjonova, seven feet tall and a future Naismith Hall of Famer, was an unstoppable force in the middle. The Soviets hadn't lost a game since 1958. A year before, at the 1975 FIBA World Championships, they were beating countries by forty points en route to the title.

And what about Team USA? Well, at that same tournament in 1975, the Americans weren't even one of the seven teams that advanced to the final round. Not much was expected of the US at these inaugural Olympic games. Expectations were so low, in fact, that what is now USA Basketball (then called ABAUSA) didn't even have a budget to send the team to Montreal. First, the team had to qualify at a pre-Olympic tournament in Hamilton, Ontario.

"So, we go there, and we end up being the gold medal team at this tournament, which means we get to go to Montreal," said Nancy Lieberman, who was the youngest member of the team at eighteen years old. In order to fly the team across Canada to the Olympics, the team's head coach, Billie Moore, along with Team USA executive director Bill Wall, put the travel on their personal credit cards. "We had to bust over there because nobody expected us to qualify," Lieberman said.

Lieberman was just one player on a roster filled with legends. She was the young gun alongside Patricia Head, who would eventually

become known as Pat Summitt, iconic coach of Tennessee. Also on the squad was UCLA star Ann Meyers, who a few years later would try out with the Indiana Pacers, and Delta State's all-world center Lusia "Lucy" Harris.

The first-ever women's Olympic basketball game was played between the US and Japan at nine a.m. "Billie Moore was having us get up at four-thirty in the morning and I was like, 'Yo, I don't get up this early,'" said Lieberman. "And

WE KNEW THE HISTORICAL SIGNIFICANCE OF WHAT WE WERE DOING.
—NANCY LIEBERMAN

Pat said, 'You will now.'" (Added Lieberman: "She was practicing coaching on me even back then.")

On that early Olympic morning, Harris scored the first points in Olympic women's basketball history; over the course of the tournament, she extended her collegiate domination to international competition, averaging fifteen points and seven rebounds a game as Team USA surprised everyone with its performance. Before the team's last game against Czechoslovakia—perhaps the only team that could hold its own with the Soviets—US head coach Billie Moore delivered a memorable pregame speech.

"We knew the historical significance of what we were doing," Lieberman said. "And this was in the locker room right before, Billie said, 'Ladies, what you do today will change the course of women's basketball history for the next twenty-five years. It will affect every little girl out there who is going to play in college or represent the United States.' And she gave this powerful locker room speech, and everyone was riveted and, son of a gun, she was right."

Twenty years later, the 1996 Olympic team—facing another inflection point for the game—took a moment to look back and honor the squad that started it all, sending each of them plaques. *Thank you for setting all this up for us,* the gesture said.

★ The team didn't even have spots in the Olympic village; all twelve ended up staying in a single two-bedroom apartment with bunk beds in the two rooms.

★ Marian Washington and Colleen Bowser were the first Black players to compete for Team USA, at the 1971 FIBA World Championships.

★ From Nancy, on Pat Summitt: "By default, I had to guard Pat every day in practice. She was five foot ten. She was country strong, and I was New York slick. The battles in practice! I was five eight and I could dunk a tennis ball; she was smarter than a professor, and I was dumber than a box of rocks, but I was athletic."

THE
BLAZE!

CAROL BLAZEJOWSKI
WINS FIRST-EVER
WADE TROPHY

By the time Carol Blazejowski was a senior at Montclair State University she was being profiled in the *New York Times* under the headline "Tomboy." The article's opening anecdote is familiar to sports-loving girls (and women!) everywhere: Carol is eleven years old and roaming the streets of her New Jersey neighborhood, basketball tucked under her arm, looking for a game. "Typical tomboy of the neighborhood," Blazejowski describes herself in the article.

This was 1968. Before Title IX—when playing sports was not yet socially acceptable for girls. But Carol was a natural. And she loved it. "I suffered a lot of verbal abuse when I was younger," she told the *Times*. "You know, 'Girls shouldn't be doing this,' the usual male chauvinist reaction. Sometimes I thought about it. But I'm so competitive I always wanted to be the best in anything. A lot of girls would have gone home, but I stayed around."

Blazejowski went to Cranford High School. No girls' basketball team existed until she spearheaded the effort just in time for her senior year—in 1974. That was two years *after* Title IX, but of course the law demanding equitable funding for women wasn't yet implemented. Men were dragging their feet. That year, her first and last playing in high school, Blazejowski led Cranford to the state championship and averaged thirty-two points per game. She was five foot ten, had a killer jumper, and wanted to keep playing in college.

She enrolled at Montclair State, just down the road. The school didn't offer athletic scholarships, but it was affordable and Blazejowski—who would be dubbed "the Blaze" in college—could major in physical education. She played all four years without a scholarship, as did all her teammates. "We'll probably be the last team ever to get to the Final Four without a scholarship player," she told the *New York Times* in 1978, during her senior season in college. The article was written the day before Montclair State traveled to Los Angeles to play UCLA, and star Ann Meyers, in the AIAW semifinals. "I just decided to come here because I knew they had a good program and because my family didn't have much money. My father's a blue-collar worker, my mother has a job in a bank. I couldn't afford to go anywhere fancy."

Maybe Montclair State wasn't "fancy," but the Blaze made it famous. It was fun, she would say, taking a school nobody had ever heard of and giving it a reputation. During her junior season, in 1977, she scored fifty-two points at Madison Square Garden in a win over Queens College. ("I didn't even realize I was setting the record," she said years later. "I was just in the

LIKE MANY HOOPERS OF THIS ERA, THE BLAZE'S CAREER FELL INTO A LITERAL NO-MAN'S LAND.

zone.") And in 1978, Blazejowski was awarded the first-ever Wade Trophy, named in honor of Delta State coach Margaret Wade and given to the best player in women's college basketball.

In women's basketball history, the 1977 doubleheader played that day at MSG is legendary. As the *Times* explained to its readers the next morning: "Women's basketball took a major leap—if not a slam-dunk—onto the American sports scene yesterday by drawing 12,336 fans to Madison Square Garden, the cradle of the collegiate doubleheader. And the place rocked as it used to when it drew large college crowds. With the leaping cheerleaders, the excitable coaches, the partisan backers— except that their voices were soprano, it looked and sounded like an old-fashioned Garden matchup."

That fifty-two-point mark? It remained the most points scored at MSG—by a man or a woman—until Kobe Bryant dropped sixty-one points against the Knicks in 2009.

Like many hoopers of this era, the Blaze's career fell into a literal no-man's land. She was the captain of the 1980 US Olympic team, only to have President Jimmy Carter boycott the games, which were held in Moscow. She then signed with the New Jersey Gems of the Women's Professional Basketball League in 1980. In her one season before the WBL folded, the Blaze was named Most Valuable Player and led the league in scoring, but she then had to sue the Gems for back pay and bonuses. And because she'd taken money, she lost her amateur status for the 1984 Los Angeles Olympics.

Even so, the Blaze is a legend—one of those players whose passion and dedication grew the game and paved the way for what (and who) came after. As she told the *New York Times* in that long-ago article, "Tomboy," she possessed a rare confidence in what she could do because she'd been doing it since she was a little kid. "I'll take what the defense gives," she said. "The major key is to be consistent. You can count on me for so many points and rebounds in a game. I know I can do it because I've worked so many hours on it. That's what it takes."

> ★ She scored 3,199 total points at Montclair State and averaged 38.6 points per game during her senior season.

THE BIRTH OF A LEAGUE

THE STORY OF THE WOMEN'S PROFESSIONAL BASKETBALL LEAGUE

On December 8, 1978, famed CBS anchorman Walter Cronkite announced the arrival of the Women's Professional Basketball League (WBL) with a four-minute, fifteen-second segment on national TV the night before the league's opening game. Bill Byrne, league founder and president, watched in a downtown Milwaukee hotel. So did other WBL executives, owners, coaches, and staff.

When Cronkite finished his piece, the room filled with applause and cheers. They'd done it. They'd made history. They'd launched the first-ever professional women's basketball league! "I think we have a good product, and I think we'll put a lot of people to work," Byrne told the *New York Times*. "What I would like the people and the press to realize is we're not men and we're not the NBA. It's an interesting game. All I ask is that people come to see one game, and I'm sure they'll come back."

The following night, the Milwaukee Does beat the Chicago Hustle in front of 7,824 people. The WBL launched in 1978 with eight franchises, each paying a $50,000 entrance fee. Byrne was an upstart sports executive who'd previously been involved in the World Football League. Byrne took note of the rise in popularity of basketball, domestically in the years after Title IX and also around the world. He figured the 1980 Moscow Olympics would serve as another springboard, with millions watching the Olympic tournament. Byrne wanted his nascent league to be ahead of that explosive moment.

Six months before the Cronkite piece, and the opening tip-off, the WBL held its first-ever draft at the Essex House in midtown Manhattan. Many of the first draft picks were skeptical of the league—for various reasons. One of the top college players, Carol "the Blaze" Blazejowski, was drafted by the New

Jersey Gems, but she wouldn't sign because she wanted to retain her amateur status for the 1980 Olympics. The Houston franchise drafted Lusia Harris, who starred at Delta State, but the former Olympian was dubious of the low salaries. Byrne estimated average players would make between $5,000 and $15,000, with stars earning possibly as much as $25,000. When reached by the *New York Times*, Harris said, "I wouldn't even consider playing for that salary. I make that, sitting here. I know the women won't play for nothing."

And so, the WBL launched without most of the game's biggest names, including UCLA's Ann Meyers. Byrne's growth plan for the league hinged on the free media attention that players would undoubtedly receive during the 1980 Olympics. He predicted that Team USA's biggest stars would come home and anchor franchises, drawing local fan interest. (The NBA would rely on this same model in launching the WNBA—aka the "W"—after the 1996 Atlanta Olympics.)

Still months before President Jimmy Carter announced the boycott, the league entered its second season with six additional franchises. New franchises were awarded to Dallas, New Orleans, St. Louis, and San Francisco. Two additional new franchises—Philadelphia and Washington—disbanded after only ten games. The New York Stars won that year's championship, just weeks after President Carter's announcement. Signs of trouble began early in the WBL's third season, with players in Minnesota staging a walkout over unpaid salaries.

Donna Orender, who played in the WBL and went on to become commissioner of the WNBA, wrote an editorial for the *New York Times* soon after the league folded in 1981. She explained the predicament, and experience, of playing in the WBL.

When the United States boycotted the Olympics, Byrne's three-year plan soon dissolved into a struggle among impoverished owners unsure of their direction, temperamental coaches, and a couple of hundred players, confused and disillusioned over missed paydays, hostile arenas and a press interested more in pin-ups than lay-ups...

In three seasons, a league identity still had not developed and the undercapitalized owners were skimping on the area they could least afford—marketing and public relations. No one promised that the W.B.L. would be an easy sell, but no one promised that it could sell itself.

I would get up some mornings and ask myself if it was all worth it...I finished my third season with the Hustle, knowing that the likelihood of a fourth season was remote...

It appears I'm a has-been now, washed up at 24.

Although the WBL folded sooner than everyone imagined, the ripple effects from the league can still be felt today. The WBL laid the groundwork for the future. It was the first viable professional league. Dozens of the WBL's best players went on to hall of fame careers, and dozens more became coaches and mentors and impacted the next generation in deep and meaningful ways. Their names (and games!) are legendary: Patricia Roberts, Charlene McWhorter Jackson, Peggie Gillom, Elizabeth McQuitter, Molly Bolin Kazmer, Adrian Mitchell-Newell, Peggy Kennedy, Retha Swindell, Debra Thomas...

Almost everything that came next can be traced back to the women of the WBL.

★ The eight inaugural teams: Chicago Hustle, Houston Angels, Iowa Cornets, Milwaukee Does, Minnesota Fillies, New Jersey Gems, New York Stars, Dayton Rockettes.

★ Forgotten stars: Brenda Chapman was the WBL's leading scorer in its inaugural season. Rita Easterling was the MVP of that first season.

★ The Houston Angels won the league's first title; the New York Stars won the second season. The Nebraska Wranglers (an expansion franchise) won the third and final title, defeating the Dallas Diamonds and star Nancy Lieberman.

★ Ann Meyers played in the second season, winning co-MVP with "Machine Gun" Molly Bolin.

$100K WOMAN

NANCY LIEBERMAN RULES THE COURT

Nancy Lieberman has the kind of swagger that comes from growing up in Queens, New York, and polishing her game on the streets, playing pickup ball against guys. So one single story can't fully capture Lieberman, but let's try anyway.

It's just before Christmas 1979, and Lieberman is a senior guard for Old Dominion, which at that time is perhaps the best women's college team the world has ever seen. The Lady Monarchs played in front of a packed house at home—they were the gold standard. "We'd walk off the court and coaches on the opposing team would whisper in my ear, *'What's it like to play every night in front of sell-out crowds? What's it like to win championships?'* And I mean, this is Geno Auriemma, this is Pat Summitt—these are people that I really admire, in awe of Old Dominion."

That year, Old Dominion is defending its national title, and Lieberman is the reigning winner of the Wade Trophy, given annually to the best player in college hoops. The Old Dominion squad is in New York City, for a holiday tournament, and Nancy pops by the set of the *Today* show with host Jane Pauley. In 1979, a new professional women's basketball league—the WBL—is in the middle of its second season, and Pauley asks the young, cocky Old Dominion guard about her future.

According to Lieberman, here's how the story goes. (On live TV!)

"Well, Nancy, are you going to play in the WBL next year?" Jane asks.

"Yeah, of course I'm going to play," Nancy responds.

"Your friend Ann Meyers is the highest paid player in the league; she makes fifty thousand dollars," Jane continues. "So where do you want to play?"

"Oh, I don't care where I play."

"Well, what will you ask for?"

"I don't know what I'm going to ask for, but I'm twice as good and twice as young, so I guess I should get a hundred thousand dollars," Nancy responds.

And she did get twice as much! She did get $100,000! The next year, after she and freshman Anne Donovan won their second consecutive national championship, Lieberman was drafted number one by the Dallas Diamonds of the WBL. Over the summer, she played in an

NBA summer league—not like today's summer leagues but still filled with NBA players. One evening, *Sports Illustrated* stopped by to check in on the spectacle of Lieberman vs. The Men. "This is going to help me become better," Lieberman told the magazine in 1980. "All through junior high and high school I played against guys, and when I got to Old Dominion, I was that much better than the other freshmen. But in college I played 80 percent of the time against women, and the gap between my ability and everyone else's seemed to narrow."

But the WBL folded the following year, and despite numerous starts and stops, another professional league for women wouldn't take root until the ABL and WNBA launched around the same time in 1996. By the WNBA's inaugural season, Lieberman was thirty-nine years old. Still, she signed on, averaging eleven minutes per game for the Phoenix Mercury.

The legend of Nancy Lieberman lives. But she is perhaps the most famous of a handful of players—Cheryl Miller and Lusia Harris among them—whose game fell into what we might call an abyss: those decades of history when the game was evolving and thriving, but there was no professional league to showcase the talent.

"I was never jealous of Rebecca Lobo, but I was like, 'She gets to play her entire career on ESPN?'" Lieberman said, referring to the former University of Connecticut star. "So many

★ Lieberman never played overseas; she always stayed around the game here—playing for the Dallas Diamonds and the Women's American Basketball Association, and in 1988 she played for the Harlem Globetrotters.

★ Connected generations! In 1993, Sheryl Swoopes hired Lieberman as her manager coming out of Texas Tech.

★ In 1998, Lieberman was hired and spent three years as the general manager and head coach of the Detroit Shock.

★ In 2015, the Sacramento Kings hired her as an assistant coach.

★ In 2018, she was hired to coach the Power in the BIG3.

of these athletes have a different platform than we did. It was very much envy because, when people are like, 'You're the best player in the world.' Well, who the hell is watching? The guys I'm playing lunch ball against? I don't want much in life, because I have more than I could ever have asked for, but I will say I would have given a little piece of my pinkie to play in my prime against some of the greatest female athletes in the world—that would have been super cool."

THREE DAYS IN INDIANA

ANN MEYERS, THE FIRST AND ONLY WOMAN TO SIGN AN NBA CONTRACT

Being the first is both exhilarating and exhausting, as Ann Meyers learned in the fall of 1979. Just a few years earlier, she'd been the first female athlete to earn a four-year scholarship, so the golden-haired UCLA hoops star was no stranger to blazing paths. But that determination would be tested after Meyers accepted an offer made during one unexpected phone call.

That call came from Sam Nassi, then the brand-new owner of the NBA's Indiana Pacers. He had an idea for Ann: she should come try out for his team. She was twenty-four years old, in the prime of her career, coming off winning the 1978 AIAW national title, and before that the silver medal in the 1976 Summer Olympics in Montreal.

Nassi's idea intrigued Meyers. She'd grown up one of eleven kids, never backing down, wanting to prove herself on every field and court she stepped on—regardless of gender. She'd also grown up dreaming of playing in the NBA. Why wouldn't she? At the time, it was the only professional basketball league that existed. And one more thing played on her mind: when she was in high school, she'd been invited to try out for the boys' team, but she'd let others talk her out of it, and she'd always wondered what might have been.

During Meyers' years at UCLA, the campus was the center of the basketball universe. Famed coach John Wooden led the men's team, which boasted legendary players such as Lew Alcindor and Bill Walton. Meyers often played pickup with them at Pauley Pavilion.

Meyers didn't take the opportunity lightly. She talked it over with her parents and siblings. Signing a contract with the Pacers meant she'd have to give up on the 1980 Los Angeles Olympics; she'd also been the top draft pick for the newly formed Women's Professional Basketball League, and she knew trying out for the Pacers instead would irk a few people.

"I wasn't going to let people talk me out of it. I thought to myself, 'I'm being offered an opportunity to play on the biggest stage, and I have to try.'"

Not everyone was a fan of the decision, or of Nassi offering the contract in the first place. That September, as word leaked out of the Pacers inviting a woman to rookie camp, a press conference was arranged in Los Angeles. Meyers had signed a one-year, $50,000 contract with Indiana. (The minimum contract back then was $140,000 a year.) A couple famous people went on the record with the *New York Times* expressing annoyance at the move.

Here, for example, is what ESPN announcer Dick Vitale, then the coach of the Detroit Pistons, told the *Times*: "I'm known as a showman, but I never would have thought up something like this. There is no way she can play at this level."

Sonny Werblin, at the time the president of Madison Square Garden, was quoted as saying, "It's utterly ridiculous. It's disgraceful. I don't think the commissioner should condone it. I think it's bad for the image of pro basketball. It's a travesty."

THE GOLDEN-HAIRED UCLA HOOPS STAR WAS NO STRANGER TO BLAZING PATHS.

SHE WASN'T GOING TO INDIANA AS SOME PR STUNT; SHE WAS GOING TO PROVE SOMETHING TO HERSELF.

THE FIRST AND ONLY WOMAN

But Meyers was focused on training. She had just six weeks to prepare for the NBA level. But perhaps even more importantly, she had to keep a distinct mindset: that she could make the team, that she belonged. "I did not watch TV, I did not listen to the radio, I did not read newspapers. I didn't want negativity."

In 1986, Hinkle Fieldhouse would be the backdrop for the famous basketball movie *Hoosiers*, but that first day of tryout was already like something from Hollywood:

cameras everywhere, following Meyers' every move. She wanted none of it. She wasn't going to Indiana as some PR stunt; she was going to prove something to herself. She was going to make the team.

Meyers was five foot nine and 135 pounds, going up against some of the strongest and fastest athletes in the world. But she did have one advantage: she was used to playing against guys, and they weren't used to playing against her.

TO SIGN AN
NBA CONTRACT

"I think during the second practice, [assistant coach Jack] McCloskey called everyone into the circle and ripped into us—salty language—but he lit into everyone, she's out here trying to get a job just like you guys, so just forget about it, let's just play. I'd been playing with guys my whole life, so I knew what guys said to you—I'd had years of preparation for this moment."

Pacers head coach Bob Leonard made the first round of cuts, and Meyers survived, but the next day, after the sixth practice of tryouts, he called Meyers into one of the classrooms. "I was sitting on a desk. He said, 'You did a good job, you worked hard, you're talented.' From there I just kind of fogged out: what I heard was, you didn't make it. I remember going back to the hotel room just devastated. I was crying my eyes out."

But today, the way Meyers sees it, failure wasn't getting cut; failure would have been not walking into that fieldhouse at all.

THE NCAA ERA BEGINS

A LEGEND-FILLED FIRST GAME

★ Hall of Famers in that '82 game: Kim Mulkey, Sonja Hogg, Gary Blair, Leon Barmore, C. Vivian Stringer.

★ Kim Mulkey went on to become (and still is) one of the best coaches in America, at Baylor and now LSU.

★ The '82 NCAA final was aired on CBS, and color commentary was by legend Ann Meyers.

★ The 9,531 seats inside "The Scope" in Norfolk were sold out for the final.

The story reads like a script: in 1974, a young Sonja Hogg gets the job of her dreams, teaching physical education at her alma mater, Louisiana Tech. The president of the school, F. Jay Taylor, asks her to stop by his office. He tells her that three female students have asked him about forming a basketball team, and would she like to start the program? Hogg tells him that's a wonderful idea, and despite not having ever played or coached, she says yes.

Dr. Taylor gives Hogg a check for $5,000. "I had about sixty-eight women show up for try-outs including some great high school basketball players," Hogg told HoopsHD. "I ordered some fabulous custom-made uniforms, and some Converse tennis shoes. I was told to have my players act like nice young ladies and that I should schedule our games on different nights than the men's games."

Hogg coached by herself for the first three seasons, going 54–28, before hiring local high school coach Leon Barmore as her assistant. With Barmore, a former state champion in high school, now in charge of in-game strategy, the Lady Techsters took off. By 1981, they were the best team in the country, going 34–0 and beating Tennessee in the AIAW championship final. "Every time Tennessee came to play us, I would send our own bus to transport Pat's team from the airport, and I gave her an extra car to use," Hogg remembered of those days. "The night before we played, our president would invite both teams over to dinner

and give her a special bottle of perfume...and then after we played Pat would come over to my house to wash the Tennessee uniforms!"

As 1981 rolled into 1982, and as the NCAA began boxing out the AIAW, the Louisiana Lady Techsters were the through line, remaining the most dominant team in America. "We were Connecticut before Connecticut," Barmore, by then Louisiana Tech's associate head coach, told the *News-Star* of Monroe, Louisiana, years later. The squad included Pam Kelly (who won that year's Wade Trophy) and Angela Turner, as well as 1984 Olympians Janice Lawrence and Kim Mulkey.

"I don't say this in a negative way, but there will never be another era like that at Louisiana Tech in women's basketball," Mulkey told the *News-Star*. "They could build the program back up, they could win another national championship, but that era was just so special, and you just can't duplicate that."

Hogg and Barmore were a unique tag team. Hogg was a genius recruiter, Barmore a

LOUISIANA TECH PLAYED WITH A SPEED NEVER SEEN BEFORE. THEY RAN. THEY PUSHED THE TEMPO. AND THEY HAD DEPTH ON THEIR ROSTER. THE COMMUNITY LOVED THEM.

fabulous in-game strategist. Also on staff was assistant coach Gary Blair, who went on to win the 2011 NCAA title with Texas A&M. And the trio, along with their players, were at the forefront of the modern game. Gone were set shots and slow, deliberate movement. (That slow pace was an artifact of the earlier restrictions on player movement in the women's game.) In were athleticism and jump shots and a fast pace. Louisiana Tech played with a speed never seen before. They ran. They pushed the tempo. And they had depth on their roster. The community loved them.

"There we sat in little ol' Ruston, Louisiana. People didn't have a whole lot to do except come out and watch the Lady Techsters play," Hogg told the *News-Star*. "I give a lot of credit to our fan base and how they followed us. They would follow us all over the country."

And in 1982, thousands followed the Lady Techsters to the campus of Old Dominion, in Virginia, site of the first-ever NCAA Final Four. Louisiana Tech would face Cheyney State, coached by a young C. Vivian Stringer, whose story at Cheyney began very much like Hogg's.

THE NCAA REIGNS SUPREME
The End of the Association for Intercollegiate Athletics for Women (AIAW)

From 1971 to 1982, the AIAW existed to govern women's sports. After the passage of Title IX, membership in the AIAW exploded, with nearly 1,000 schools at its peak. The AIAW organized women's college sports in the same way the National Collegiate Athletic Association (NCAA) oversaw men's sports. In fact, the NCAA first wanted nothing to do with women's sports, and even raised money to file lawsuits *against* Title IX, attempting to limit the protections guaranteed by its passage. But after a decade of (at least decent) funding, the NCAA realized Title IX was here to stay. Rather than allowing the AIAW, run by women, to govern women's sports, the NCAA made a move. It wanted power and control.

At the 1981 national meeting, NCAA schools held a contentious vote. Should the NCAA sponsor Division I women's championships? If the motion passed, the AIAW would effectively be killed. And the difference between the AIAW and the NCAA was profound: the AIAW was dedicated solely to women's sports; the NCAA had at times aligned itself against women's sports.

At that national meeting, the motion was initially defeated (by one vote). But another vote was called, some lobbying took place, the motion was passed, and the NCAA launched into women's sports. For the 1981–82 school year, member institutions could compete in both the AIAW and NCAA championships. By 1982, it was one or the other. And by 1983, the AIAW ceased to exist.

AIAW CHAMPIONS

1972: Immaculata	1978: UCLA
1973: Immaculata	1979: Old Dominion
1974: Immaculata	1980: Old Dominion
1975: Delta State	1981: Louisiana Tech
1976: Delta State	1982: Rutgers [*]
1977: Delta State	

Split season when many teams competed in the first-ever NCAA championship.

CHEYNEY STATE MAKES HISTORY
The Only HBCU to Reach the NCAA Final Four

"Not a dime," Stringer told *Sports Illustrated* about how much money she made coaching the women's basketball team at Cheyney State, a historically Black university in Pennsylvania. "I never got paid. I was just grateful to have the opportunity."

The former Rutgers coach started at Cheyney in 1971, as an associate professor of health and physical education, and volunteered to coach the basketball team. She was twenty-two years old. In those early years, the school competed in Division II, but Stringer scheduled games against bigger local competition, teams like Rutgers and Penn State. Her classroom doubled as the team's locker room, and they'd often bus back after games to save the hotel costs. Stringer explained to *SI*, "We were poor, but we never held that against us. We never felt sorry for us. Because we didn't have anything, we feared no one and I think that was the greatest motivation in the world."

The men's team at Cheyney was coached by John Chaney, who would go on to spend twenty-four seasons at Temple and in 2001 was inducted into the Basketball Hall of Fame. Because there was only one gym, and resources were limited, the two coaches—Chaney and Stringer—often coached both teams together.

By the 1981–82 season, the small Pennsylvania school was Division I, and boasting a stacked roster including Debra Walker and Yolanda Lacey, as well as the only Division I coaching staff of all Black women. The Lady Wolves were also inspired by the struggle of Stringer's young daughter, Janine, who had been hospitalized that November with spinal meningitis.

In the first-ever NCAA tournament, Cheyney State defeated Auburn, North Carolina State, Kansas State, and Maryland—a quartet of programs with more money and prestige. But the Lady Wolves were playing for something bigger. Here's a snippet of the story from the *Philadelphia Inquirer*'s Mel Greenberg on the morning of the NCAA final:

NORFOLK, Va.—Cheyney State's women's basketball team gets to play one of the leading roles on a new CBS television program today (Channel 10, noon). It's called "40 Minutes." That's how close the second-ranked Lady Wolves (28–2) are to winning the first NCAA Division I women's title. All coach Vivian Stringer has to do is figure out how to use that time to outscore Louisiana Tech (34–1), the nation's No. 1 team for the past 36 weeks.

The game will be played before an expected sellout crowd of about 10,000 at the Scope...

Tech, a decided favorite, is making its fourth straight appearance in a national final under coach Sonja Hogg. The previous three were in the Association for Intercollegiate Athletics for Women tournament, where Louisiana Tech won last year's title.

The Lady Techsters were a deep team. Famously, Summitt quipped about Louisiana Tech, "I've always said they have the two best teams in America." After leading early in the game, Cheyney State couldn't contend with the Lady Techsters' steady march of talent, and the Lady Wolves lost, 76–62.

Yet still, history was made. And that night when the Cheyney team returned to campus, at just past midnight, the student body was there to greet them, encircling the team bus and blasting music. "If there were 2,000 students on campus that weekend then 1,999 were lined up waiting to greet us," Walker told *SI*. "That just showed how historic that moment was."

CHERYL MILLER,
CYNTHIA COOPER,
AND PAM AND
PAULA MCGEE

RUN
LOS ANGELES

⚡

They were Showtime, the female Lakers, a team of future legends—a handful of the greatest players of all time!—suiting up for the University of Southern California in the early 1980s.

Cheryl Miller. Cynthia Cooper. Pam and Paula McGee. Rhonda Windham. Coach Linda Sharp. The media, from coast to coast, wanted sit-down interviews with them. Or, if that was too big an ask, could they at least have a phoner? The campus was abuzz; fans packed the stands. This team was lit. "We were huge," Miller said. "We were just huge."

And did they know it?

"Just a little bit," said the Hall of Famer, smirking. "Yeah, just a little bit. You're young,

you know? And getting lavished with so much praise."

In 1982, Cheryl Miller was the most sought-after high school recruit in the country. She was six foot two, with a silky smooth jump shot, and she could dunk. Her brother, NBA legend Reggie Miller, who was two years younger, was present the first time Cheryl threw down. He relayed the moment to the *New York Times* back in 1983: "We were playing in our front-yard driveway, and all of a sudden she just said she could feel it coming, and she got a good running start, and she just did it."

Miller wasn't sure which college to pick. Should she go to UCLA, with former Olympic coach Billie Moore, and alma mater of her idol, Ann Meyers? Or should she say yes to USC, and Sharp, who called her every day—recruiting rules didn't yet exist—and talked to Miller about everything *except* hoops?

Sharp told the twins, sophomores Pam and Paula McGee, that Miller was still on the fence about where to play her college ball. So, one afternoon, the duo drove to Miller's home in Riverside, California, to have lunch with the prized recruit. "We were sitting on the couch," Miller said, remembering that long-ago day. "Paula was on my right; Pam was on my left. I noticed they were getting closer and closer to where they were squeezing me. And then Pam goes, 'Look, we're trying to do something important here; we're trying to do something big.' And Paula was like, 'Pam, be quiet. Miller, let me just say this: you can either play two years with us, or two years against us.' I said, 'Where do I sign?' And that was it."

For the women of Troy, the games were easier than the practices. The unwritten rule, for this team comfortable with the glitz and glamour and hype, was *once we're inside the gym: it's all focus.* Coach Sharp wasn't a yeller. And she never lashed out. "But because we were so close to her, she laid that mom guilt on

MILLER AND COMPANY WERE SUCH A *THING* THAT THEY PLAYED *AFTER* THE USC MEN'S BASKETBALL TEAM.

you. That whole, 'I'm so *disappointed* in you.' She was brilliant."

Every two weeks or so, the McGee twins would get into some sort of heated argument and need to be separated. And Miller and Cynthia Cooper, a future two-time WNBA MVP, they had *history*. "I was always getting into it with Cynthia because we played against each other in high school," Miller said. "She was from LA, so she had that bounce and everything else, and I grew up in Riverside, which was considered Mayberry. They used to make fun of me, but I always kicked her butt in high school. Then we're on the same team, and there is still that animosity. So, we had our issues."

But once the lights went up, they all had a vibe. "It was like that old adage: you can beat up on your brother and sister," Miller said. "But God forbid anyone else touch them."

Few teams could. In Miller's freshman season, the Trojans won the NCAA title over Louisiana Tech, finishing the season 31–2. The freshman sensation played all forty minutes in the final, scored twenty-seven points, and had nine rebounds, four blocked shots, and four steals. "I don't think she played like a freshman," Sharp, presumably deadpan, told the media members that day. The next season, with the same star-studded roster, USC beat burgeoning Tennessee and head coach Pat Head Summitt for their second consecutive title.

Miller and Company were such a *thing* that they played *after* the USC men's basketball team. "We used to give our men a hard time, because they played before us," Miller said. "We were the team that everybody came to watch. And Cooper, she was always yapping. We would come running out and they're coming off the court after the game and she's like, 'Hey guys, thanks for warming up the court for us!' And I'm like, 'Oh my gosh, Coop, c'mon now.' But that's how it was."

Yup, that's exactly how it was.

"To this day, people come up to me and say, 'I remember when,'" said Miller. "I have so many *I remember when*s. I am blessed and fortunate—I have no idea why—but people still remember. People who never saw me play, for some reason, they almost talk to me as if I'm still playing."

★ Reggie Miller, in 1983, told the *New York Times* that at first having a famous sister irked him a little. "I didn't like hearing, 'Oh, you're Miller's brother' all the time. I wanted to make my own name. But then I realized it helped make people notice me more, and so I don't mind it at all now."

★ Miller was the first player, man or woman, to be named All-American by *Parade* magazine all four years of high school.

★ *Women of Troy* is a documentary film that premiered in 2020.

★ Lisa Leslie starred at USC from 1990 to 1994 and won the 1994 Naismith Award.

Cheryl Miller is a vibe!

That's right. You start to see the swagger coming into the game.

I think I'm gonna steal this move when I get that ring this year – sitting on the rim, crossed-legged.

THE GOLDEN GIRLS

USA WINS FIRST-EVER OLYMPIC GOLD

Pat Summitt did not like Cheryl Miller. During the college basketball season, this was perfectly fine, even expected. Miller was the six-foot-two star at the University of Southern California, which in 1984 defeated Summitt's Tennessee squad for its second consecutive NCAA title. So the dynamic made sense: no love lost between these two competitors.

But during the summer, Summitt was the head coach of Team USA. Miller was its star. And the two just weren't feeling each other. Maybe it had something to do with the cartwheel that Miller had executed in front of the Lady Vols' bench after beating them for the championship. *Maybe.* "I was still on the court, but I just did a cartwheel and jumped up into the arms of one of my teammates," Miller said. "I didn't know that Pat had been watching the whole thing. So, fast-forward to the Olympics..."

Ahead of the 1984 Summer Games, the team was in Taiwan for the Jones Cup, a warm-up tournament before the main attraction. Miller vividly remembered one game. She was playing as poorly as she can remember. "I'm having the worst game I've ever played," Miller said. "And I'm talking from kindergarten, the worst ever. I couldn't even make a layup!"

At halftime, Summitt lined up everyone in the locker room and proceeded to verbally undress each player. That is, each player except, conspicuously, Miller. As Summitt sent everyone back out to the court, Miller

remembered thinking, *Woah, thank you, Jesus.* But as the players filed out of the room, Summitt called, "Oh, wait, wait, wait, I forgot one special person!"

Miller froze. *Oh, here we go, here we go,* she thought.

In front of the team, Summitt walked over to Miller and barked, "Cheryl Miller, let me tell you something. I will win or lose a gold medal *without you*!"

"The one thing that I knew she wanted to do was make me cry, and that's the last thing I was going to let happen," Miller said. "She had made certain people on our team—I won't mention names—cry, and I was like, I'm not going to be the one. But let me tell you, I was quivering."

A few minutes later, Miller jogged onto the court for the start of the second half, but Summitt stopped her, told her to sit down. She was benched for the second half.

The following week, Summitt held coach-player meetings, and when it was Miller's turn she walked into the office and sat across from the young, fiery head coach. After the standard back-and-forth, Summitt paused and said, "Can I ask you a question?"

"It's your room, you're the coach," Miller responded.

"Why do you have to be so flamboyant?" Summitt asked.

"What do you mean *flamboyant*?" Miller said, slightly taken aback. And Summitt proceeded to mention a few things she had noticed, such as dancing, chest-bumping, jumping around, maybe...*cartwheeling*. Miller remembered Summitt saying, "If you make a good play why can't you just make a good play and leave it alone? Why do you have to do all this... extra?"

Miller responded that she wasn't being "extra"; she just played with emotion. "That's just how I play," Miller said. "I don't see a lot

★ That year's team was: Teresa Edwards, Lea Henry, Lynette Woodard, Anne Donovan, Cathy Boswell, Miller, Janice Lawrence, Cindy Noble, Kim Mulkey, Denise Curry, Pamela McGee, and Carol Menken-Schaudt.

★ The USSR boycotted the 1984 Games, and the Russians were the Americans' only real competition. Team USA ended up not even being challenged; its closest game was the gold medal win over Korea, which they won, 85–55.

★ "The game was played before a crowd of 11,280 in the 17,000-seat Forum. The ticket prices, ranging from $40 to $95, are the same as the prices for the men's final Friday night. At the time the tickets went on sale, there was the anticipation of a possible gold-medal game between the United States and the Soviet Union."—*New York Times*, August 8, 1984.

of emotion from you, so I'm just trying to help you out, too. So that's why I get excited about playing, and that's not going to change. And if that's an issue with you, yeah, you can bench me, but I will tell you this, Coach Summitt: you won't win a gold medal without me.'"

Then Miller got up and walked out of the room. And what happened next is the key—not just to how Team USA went on to win the gold medal that long-ago summer, but the key to how Summitt went on to become the legendary, timeless coach she did. She didn't dig in her heels. She listened to Miller. "I think when she found out that it was genuine, and it wasn't me trying to belittle anyone, or make myself bigger than the game, that it was just the emotion and the excitement in how I played, she saw that, realized it, and I think that's when her wall came down," Miller said. "And her opinions about me, they basically dissolved."

Miller wore a gold cross necklace, a gift from her mom. And for the rest of that summer, before Miller went onto the court, she'd take off the necklace and put it around Summitt's neck. "And we ended up being very, very tight," Miller said. "Very close."

That summer, Team USA was preparing for another epic clash with the Soviet Union, which had beaten the Americans on a last-second shot to win the 1983 World Championships. But early in the summer, the USSR announced it would be boycotting the Olympics. The decision

disappointed Miller and the rest of the squad: they wanted a rematch, they wanted to beat the best.

Instead, they demolished the competition. No other country could touch them. "I just remember the gold medal being placed around my neck and I remember seeing my mom in the stands and I could see her crying and my dad holding her and Reggie was on the other side, holding her. Then I walked off the podium to my mom in the stands and I placed the medal around her neck. Her nickname for me was Pearl, and she goes, 'Pearl, you did it.' And I said, 'No, we did it.' And so now we're all crying. It was awesome."

TROTTING THE GLOBE

THE LEGEND LYNETTE WOODARD HOOPS FOR HARLEM

When Lynette Woodard was a little kid growing up in Kansas, her cousin stopped by for dinner. This was the early 1960s, and her cousin was famous Harlem Globetrotter Hubert Ausbie. That night, Ausbie showed Lynette a few tricks, spinning a basketball on his finger. She was mesmerized. "It was unreal," Woodard told *Sports Illustrated* in a piece written twenty years later, in 1985. "I couldn't believe the magnificent things he was doing with a basketball."

It was this moment that planted the seed. Maybe someday *she* could become a Globetrotter. The famous traveling squad, started in 1926, had never had a woman before. But no matter.

Woodard worked on her game, inside the house and out. In her Wichita neighborhood, she became a staple on the playgrounds—often serving as captain for the all-male pickup games. And as a sophomore at Wichita North High School, she led the team to the 5A state championship in 1975. Two years later, she became an All-American. The next fall, the five-foot-eleven-inch guard was starting for the University of Kansas.

Woodard dominated the college game. In many ways, she was ahead of her time. She could play all five positions during an era when most players were locked into guard-forward-center. Woodard's time with the Jayhawks came before the NCAA governed women's basketball—it was still the AIAW—so she's not technically the NCAA's all-time leading scorer. But that's just semantics. She is the leading scorer in women's college basketball history, dropping 3,649 points during her four-year career, which ended in 1981. "She's a real pioneer of women's basketball," WNBA all-star Cappie Pondexter told the *New York Times* years later. "She's graced the game with her abilities when a lot of people didn't play like her."

Woodard made the 1980 US Olympic team, which was sidelined by President Jimmy Carter's decision to boycott the Moscow Games. Like many young athletes, Woodard had been an aspiring Olympian since she was a kid. In a story in the *Cleveland Plain-Dealer*, Woodard's older brother Darrell remembers how the two kids would shoot rolled-up socks over open doors and use the stove timer as a game clock. "We used to play all kinds of games and pretend

it was the Olympics," he said. "Two pieces of candy would be the gold medal. Lynette would always win. I knew then she was ready for the Olympics."

And by 1984, she was. Now even more mature—she'd played a season in northern Italy—Woodard was named captain of the Olympic team that starred Cheryl Miller, was coached by Pat Head Summitt, and would win the country's first-ever gold medal in women's basketball. Ahead of the Los Angeles Games, Summitt told the *New York Times* that she would have been "really frightened to think [Lynette] wasn't going to be with us, going into the opening game. She's really just matured tremendously on and off the court."

After the Olympics, Woodard went back to her alma mater and became an assistant coach. It was during that next year that the Globetrotters announced their intention to add a woman to the roster. The club's president, Dick Palmer, told the *Los Angeles Times*, "Like everyone else, we were glued to the TV set during the Olympics and saw all the really good, strong women athletes," Palmer said. "The Harlem Globetrotters have had many firsts during the years, so we thought we would have another."

A few days later, the same paper reached Woodard at Kansas. "I read in the paper that the Harlem Globetrotters were looking for a female for next season," she told the paper.

"And I thought to myself, this is the female. That's the only thing that would draw me away from coaching at Kansas. I would love it, and it's serious for me. That would be the ultimate. I'm still practicing. They do a lot of wizardry with the ball, and I've always worked on that type of thing since high school."

The Globetrotters brought in eighteen women to fill one spot, but none were better suited than Woodard: she was the oldest, with the most impressive credentials, and she had a family connection to the team's lineage. And leading up to the final tryout of just ten players, Woodard trained like an Olympian. She woke up at five a.m. to lift weights and run.

Lynette Woodard as a Globetrotter. It was a no-brainer. "I got the chance of the century," she told *Sports Illustrated* in 1985. "It's the first time in history it's been done. Since the earth was created, let alone when basketball began. How sweet it is! How sweet it is!"

Woodard toured with the team for two seasons. Then ownership changed. But she kept playing—first overseas and then, finally, at the tail end of her career, in the WNBA.

★ Kansas first fielded a varsity women's basketball team in the 1968–69 season.

★ Marian Washington was the head coach at Kansas for thirty-one seasons, including all of Lynette's, from 1973 to 2004.

★ Since Woodard was the first woman to play for the Globetrotters, they've had thirteen women play for them.

★ Woodard is the only woman to *twice* be inducted into the Naismith Basketball Hall of Fame: once for her career, once with the Globetrotters.

★ Tamika Catchings, Tennessee and WNBA star, told the *New York Times*: "I wouldn't be here if it weren't for players like her."

★ Woodard played one season each with the Cleveland Rockers and the Detroit Shock before retiring from basketball for good in 1999.

 WOODARD DOMINATED THE COLLEGE GAME. IN MANY WAYS, SHE WAS AHEAD OF HER TIME. SHE COULD PLAY ALL FIVE POSITIONS.

EURO LIFE

LIVING AND LOVING THE GAME...ALL THE WAY ACROSS THE POND

The stories of playing basketball overseas border on unbelievable. WNBA legend Seimone Augustus once rode in a plane where the pilot didn't have GPS—instead, he was consulting a foldable map. This isn't even the wackiest moment that Augustus remembers. During the season, the teams travel across Europe, and beyond, in buses, cars, trains, planes, and, every so often, a ferry.

The women's game was formally established in Italy in 1930, with the Lega Basket Femminile; then in 1958, the EuroLeague started, which is still the most competitive foreign league. (The WNBA is still by far the most competitive in the world.) After some early dominance by clubs out of Bulgaria and Latvia, European teams began recruiting American players to bolster their local rosters. And by the eighties and early nineties, most European clubs had at least one American star.

In fact, let's tell the story of these early years through two of the game's biggest stars. First, Lynette Woodard, the all-time leading scorer in women's college basketball history. After playing at Kansas, she left the United States and spent the 1981–82 season in northern Italy, for a team in the town of Schio. She was the only English-speaking player. And the town didn't have a language school.

When Woodard first arrived, she thought, *Lord, what have I done?* No cell phones. No internet. Nothing but old-fashioned snail mail and expensive long-distance dialing. "It was like I was a baby," Woodard told the *New York Times* a few years after coming home. "I just had to listen hard, just try to feel my way around. It was a survival course."

The star believed the year abroad helped her mature, in the way all difficult life experiences can. A decade later, she would play three seasons in Japan.

Cynthia Cooper, one of the greatest players in history, built an entire career overseas. She graduated from the University of Southern California in 1986. After spending one season flying below the radar in Spain, making just $20,000, she signed with Basket Parma, in Italy—the birthplace of Parmesan cheese— and dominated for the next decade.

Here, let's let Cooper explain those early days overseas. This is what she wrote for the *Players' Tribune* about her years in Europe:

So as far as my career overseas goes, it's all love. But love is complicated, you know what I mean? And I think I felt some of that over the course of my run in Europe. I think there were times where maybe I'd be coming off a fifty-point game or something, or I'd hit two free throws in OT with zeros on the clock for the win, or I'd dominate a big rival, and it would just kind of hit me, like...damn, I have to admit, it would have been nice to do that with 20,000 people chanting my name. Or it would have been nice to be on SportsCenter for some highlights, or in the sports section of the LA Times the next morning with a write-up. Or it would have been nice to know that any of my people back home had really any idea at all about the levels I was reaching on this other side of the world.

And so, I wouldn't say I felt cheated out of anything, necessarily—but I still definitely had these moments where I was aware of what I was missing out on, just by virtue of being a female player instead of a male player, and where I'd think to myself, you know...wouldn't that be nice.

The isolation, especially for this first generation of hoop muses, played a large role in the overall experience. The language barriers, the time difference, the pre-smartphone era, the toiling away in isolation—all of it created a challenging experience, often plagued with homesickness.

But through it all was that kernel of realization: these women were getting paid to play basketball. They were professional basketball players.

The game overseas continued to grow. New

clubs stepped onto the world stage, specifically the ones in Russia and Turkey. The money continued to grow, too. That first season Cynthia Cooper played in Spain, for $20,000? Soon the biggest American stars were making ten times that, then twenty times, eventually even fifty times as much, and with unprecedented perks.

Seimone Augustus played seasons in Istanbul, for a famous club called Galatasaray SK, as well as in Moscow, for a club called Dynamo. Her first season overseas was in 2006, back when you had to bring DVDs for entertainment, and the main way to communicate was through Skype. She lived in modest flats, often moving during the season for one reason or another, but mostly because of the inferior quality of the rental apartment. While most people packed bags of clothes for overseas, Augustus packed food, because so much of what she wanted wasn't available in parts of Russia. "Everything was challenging. I remember hanging stuff on the laundry line to dry, just like the locals, and leaving two days before a game because so many places were hard to get to. We'd be in charge of our own uniforms, and sneakers on the road, too. Plus, it was small stuff you wouldn't think about, like we didn't have heat packs, and the ice we had

for our knees was like the ice you'd have in a kitchen freezer, in trays."

And yet, almost every player who's gone to play abroad deeply respects the experience: learning a different culture, pushing themselves outside their comfort zone, remembering always that no matter the challenge and distance and homesickness and language barrier, they're fighting for the future of the game—all across the world.

25TH AND DIAMOND

DAWN STALEY FROM PHILLY TO THE PINNACLE

n the late 1980s, Dawn Staley's high school coach in Philadelphia chirped at her, "Sometimes you're too unselfish for the good of the team. It's not called *passing* ball, it's called *basket*ball."

But Staley had grown up on the North Philly playgrounds, on the same courts as male legends Hank Gathers and Bo Kimble, and passing was what she loved best. Dishing the rock? That skill earned her respect. She loved passing. Staley was one of five kids—three boys and two girls—and the court at 25th and Diamond helped shape her. Shy by nature, basketball was her self-expression.

"I don't think I'm normal," Staley told ESPN's Allison Glock in 2020. "I'm socially inept. I still don't have very many friends. As a kid, I was really closed. Quiet. I expressed myself through my game. I thought that should be good enough for people to understand."

The boys could be cruel at first. They'd say all the age-old things like, "Get back in the kitchen!" But the more Staley passed, the more they realized she was fun to play with. She made them better. "That gave me the heart to play against anybody," Staley told *Sports Illustrated* in a 1990 profile while playing at the University of Virginia. "I'm glad they were rough. Guys seem to be born with basketball skills. Girls have to work to develop these skills. I don't know why. I do know basketball is my only fun. Nothing else ever interested me."

The five-foot-six-inch guard was feisty and endlessly creative on both ends of the court. Everywhere she went, she scrapped and clawed. And she made every team better. In college, she led the Cavaliers to three Final Fours and one national title game appearance. She was the two-time Naismith Player of the Year. At the time, UVA seemed to be the pinnacle. But this was just one stop on Staley's iconic basketball journey. She went on to win a gold medal with the transformative 1996 Olympic team, then two more in 2000 and 2004, and played eight seasons in the newly formed WNBA.

What makes Staley legendary, though, is her second act. She is the only person to win the Naismith Award as both a player *and* a coach.

IF PEOPLE THOUGHT IT COULDN'T BE DONE, SHE WANTED TO DO IT.

Even the story of her hiring at Temple in 2000 perfectly reflects Staley.

"Not one ounce of me wanted to coach," she told *USA Today* of Temple's pursuit of her in 2000. "They kept asking and asking and asking and I was saying, 'No, no, no.'"

Temple's then–athletic director, Dave O'Brien, convinced Staley to come to campus. Just visit. The school was a stone's throw from her childhood home, so no big deal. "He walks me into a conference room and there are twelve people sitting at the table and they start firing these questions at me," Staley relayed to *USA Today*. "That was their search committee. They're asking me, 'Where do you see yourself in five years?' I have no idea. They asked if I saw myself as a coach. I said, 'No, not at all.' I don't know how they left that room thinking I was the person for the job."

Staley was still playing. She was only in the first couple seasons of her WNBA career. But O'Brien knew how to push her buttons, continuing to pester her about how she would elevate the Temple program. And her US Olympic teammates and former college coach, Debbie Ryan, also motivated her, saying there was no chance she could play *and* coach. "Just my little bit of doubt there made her think, 'Oh, OK, I'm taking this job,'" Ryan said. "I always knew how to get her to do something."

As it always had, that bit of doubt stoked Staley's competitive fire. If people thought it couldn't be done, she wanted to do it. For six years, Staley coached at Temple while playing in the W. "We had to do it differently in recruiting," she said. "Instead of me saying, 'I'm going to come see you play in July,' it was, 'Why don't you come see me play?' You can spin it how you need to spin it, but we had such great relationships with our players. They were closer to me in age and followed the WNBA, so they were probably more in awe of me being their coach, and they played for that. They wanted to impress me."

In eight seasons at Temple, Staley led the Owls to six NCAA tournament appearances. Then in 2008, South Carolina came calling. Staley's parents had moved to Philly from South Carolina as teenagers in the 1950s, so she had roots there. And she wanted a new challenge.

In the decade-plus, Staley has turned the Gamecocks into a dynasty. They've so far won two NCAA titles (2017, 2022), making her the first Black coach to ever win more than one.

And South Carolina is perpetually atop the national rankings. Shockingly, the question now on the table: is Dawn Staley a better coach than she was a player?

Come to think of it, Staley's influence on the game is even wider and deeper. She might very well be the most influential person in women's basketball. Over the years, the shy kid from North Philly has grown into a fierce ambassador. People tune into Staley not *just* to watch her team, but also to hear what she has to say—even to see what she might wear. Staley's sideline fashion has become iconic. She wore a Louis Vuitton letterman jacket and matching sneakers to coach the 2022 national title game, and she has no intention of going back to heels and suits. (And nobody wants her to.)

"I'm indebted to the game, I owe basketball," Staley told espnW. "I mean, look at me. But I started playing because I needed an outlet. I was extremely competitive, probably dangerously competitive. I didn't like losing. And some of that still is very well in me."

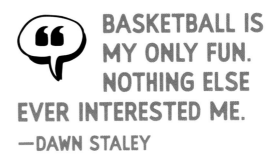

BASKETBALL IS MY ONLY FUN. NOTHING ELSE EVER INTERESTED ME.
—DAWN STALEY

THE SHOT HEARD ROUND THE WORLD

CHARLOTTE SMITH

The story we like to tell about game-winning shots is that the shooter never had a moment of doubt, that they were locked in and ready. The pressure...what pressure? We like to imagine a feeling of weight-lessness, of destiny.

Then there's the experience of Charlotte Smith, whose game-winning shot in the 1994 NCAA title game is the stuff of legend—and, if you look deeper, of life lessons. Let's let the venerable *New York Times* set the stage, with their article, "A Shot That Catches Nothing But History." It begins, "What can you do in seven-tenths of a second? If you're a world-class runner, you can run 7 or 8 yards. If you're a world-class swimmer, you can cover 5 yards. If you're the North Carolina women's basketball team, you can win the national championship."

But before we get to that final fraction of a second, let's pull back and look at the whole. The day was April 3, 1994, the location was a sold-out arena in Richmond, Virginia, and the two teams vying for the title were the North Carolina Tar Heels and the Lady Techsters of Louisiana Tech. Our eventual hero, Charlotte Smith, was having a miserable day shooting. The first half, nothing was falling—she scored only one point!—and so she said to herself, *OK, the least I can do is be a great defender and rebounder.* (She would finish with twenty-three of them; still a Final Four record.) The lesson: it's not how you start; it's how you finish.

And Smith finished with gusto, scoring nineteen of her twenty points in the second half. But the beginning of the moment—no, *the minutes*—that would change her life started when she desperately dove onto the court with teammate Marion Jones. Her team, the Tar Heels, were down a basket and the ball was loose under the rim, the clock ticking away its final seconds. Finally, the whistle blew, and the clock stopped. A jump ball had been called, and the possession arrow favored North Carolina. From the ground, Smith looked up at the scoreboard:

0.7 seconds.

When she saw that number, barely a number at all, her heart sank. "I knew in my soul the game was over and a flood of emotions came over me—my entire body, full disappointment. We had worked so hard and it was over and I'm thinking, 'What can possibly happen in point-seven seconds?" Even though her team had the ball (and so, technically, *a chance*), Smith walked to the huddle, checked out. She was physically present, but mentally absent as coach Sylvia Hatchell drew up a play. A minute later, when the Tar Heels couldn't inbound the ball because of Louisiana Tech's strong defense, Hatchell called her team's last

FROM THE GROUND, SMITH LOOKED UP AT THE SCOREBOARD: 0.7 SECONDS.

timeout. She gathered her players and dramatically changed course. And here Smith would learn another life lesson: sometimes in life you have to make gutsy decisions and gutsy moves.

Hatchell told her team, "We're going for the win, not the tie."

Down two points, Hatchell began drawing up a play for a three-pointer. Smith figured this play would be for someone else; on the season, she was only shooting 20 percent from beyond the arc. "When she chose me, my heart sank," Smith said. "Sometimes people can see in you what you don't even see in yourself. And so, I started thinking, 'If she's confident in me, I have to be confident in myself.'"

The Tar Heels walked back onto the court to set up the final play that their coach had drawn up. Smith was so nervous she couldn't remember what she was supposed to do. She whispered to her teammate Sylvia Crawley, "What are we running?" and Sylvia reminded her. A moment later, the referee handed the ball to the Tar Heels' inbound passer, who was just a foot in front of Smith. Right away,

Smith darted to screen for Tonya Sampson, the team's star, who everyone in the sold-out arena assumed was getting the ball—including the defense. Three of Louisiana Tech's players went with Tonya, and Smith could feel how open she was. She quickly backed out to behind the three-point line. "I'm actually thinking, 'I'm so nervous. Wow. I'm either going to win or lose the national title for my team.'"

And then the ball is coming toward her. An eternity unfolds, waiting for the inbound pass to arrive. Fear, prayers, nervousness course through Smith's body. She catches the ball and quickly releases it, with just two-tenths of a second to spare. "When I let go, I felt like it was a good release," Smith said. "Once the ball was in the air, everything started happening faster—I'd done all my thinking and worrying before—and there didn't even seem to be time to watch the ball in flight."

Standing just a few feet behind Smith on the sideline, Sylvia Hatchell knew the ball was good the minute it left Smith's hands. And she was right: the ball dropped through the rim. The bench leaped in celebration. The team rushed Smith and buried her in joy. "It's a moment that reminds me to never give up, to always believe in the beauty of your dream," she said.

And here's the final life lesson: sometimes people who do amazing things are terrified, and yet they do them anyway.

SLIDING DOORS

ORIGIN OF THE FIRST-EVER TENNESSEE VS. UCONN GAME ON ESPN

The year was 1994, early summer, and a woman named Carol Stiff was in charge of programming the upcoming basketball season for ESPN. The TV media giant was based out of Bristol, Connecticut, just about an hour from the UConn campus. In essence, Stiff was responsible for tracking college teams, predicting which would be good in a given year, and scheduling games between them to put on ESPN's airwaves. One game time in particular was paramount: the afternoon of Martin Luther King Day, a national holiday, when kids were home from school and adults from work.

Stiff had been paying particular attention to the team just down the road in Storrs, Connecticut. The year before, the Huskies had surprised everyone by advancing to the Elite Eight, eventually losing to North Carolina, who went on to win the title. That UConn team was young; they were bringing everyone back: Rebecca Lobo, Jamelle Elliot, Jennifer Rizzotti, Kara Wolters. Plus, the Huskies now had highly-ranked freshman recruit Nykesha Sales.

The game that Stiff needed to schedule—to be played at one p.m. on ESPN—also needed to be played at the home arena of a Big East school, per the contracts the conferences had signed with ESPN. Stiff knew this was a hurdle. Not many head coaches would be willing to take a game against UConn, on UConn's home floor. But she had her pitch ready, and Stiff decided her first call would be to Sylvia Hatchell, head coach of the Tar Heels, the defending national champs and the team that had ousted UConn in the previous year's NCAA tournament.

"I called Sylvia Hatchell and said, 'Hey, would you take this game? It's gonna be on Martin Luther King, it's gonna be on ESPN, Robin Roberts calling it—what do you think?' And I just laid out and waited for her response. A second later, she said, 'I'll play the game, but only if it's at Chapel Hill.'"

Stiff paused, then responded: "Well, maybe a year later we could do that, but, no, this year it has to be at the Big East school, at UConn—it has to be."

Hatchell held firm: she didn't want the game. Stiff tried one last time, "ESPN? One o'clock...you sure?"

No, came the response, and so Stiff thanked Coach Hatchell and moved on. She already had an idea for who she would call next, so she wasted no time.

"I called Pat Summitt, and I delivered the same exact script: 'Hey, Pat, I got this game, this window, has to be at a Big East school, and I think UConn is going to be pretty good. I know

it's January and you'll be in your SEC schedule with tough games all around it, but, ESPN, Robin Roberts calling the game...what do you think?'"

"Geez, Carol, I don't know," came Summitt's response. "I'm playing Auburn, you know, just before, then I gotta fly up to Hartford and that's really tough."

Silence filled the line, but Stiff didn't say a word, allowed the legendary Tennessee coach to process the information, to run through scenarios. Allowed her, maybe, to see the bigger picture. A beat later, Summitt's voice filled the line:

Yes, I'll do it...

For the good of the game.

Nearly nine months later, it's mid-January, the day of the matchup, and Tennessee is the number one team in the country; UConn is number two. Until this game, UConn was the pesky upstart, the rural Connecticut team still trying to prove itself. Tennessee, meanwhile, is royalty—with Summitt as its venerable and intimidating leader.

Gampel Pavilion is sold out; the *New York Times* is in the building. As promised, Robin Roberts is calling the game. That week's national poll has been held, pending the outcome of this showdown. The energy in the arena is buzzing, and around the country people are turning on ESPN in unprecedented numbers. It's not just the clash between number one and number two that piques people's interest, it's the dichotomy between the two teams— different in almost every way. The Southern dynasty of Tennessee versus the Northern newcomer; the brashness of UConn coach Geno Auriemma versus the regal Summitt.

It is everything ESPN could have hoped for, and a million people watch the game, watch the Huskies plant their flag as contenders, winning 77–66 and dog-piling at center court as Roberts makes the call: "History is made, and number one UConn now takes over!" The energy in the arena is electric. Stiff is in the press area as Auriemma walks to the podium. He is elated: *what a great game for women's basketball,* etc., etc.

The Huskies went undefeated that season, 35–0, winning the program's first national championship. They were enshrined on the cover of *Sports Illustrated*, inspiring the next generation of young talent to consider Storrs as one of the preeminent destinations to play their college ball.

Maybe it all would have ended the same, no matter what Pat Summitt had said on the phone call six months prior. We'll never know.

What we do know is that afternoon, Stiff left the press area and walked toward the Tennessee locker room. She didn't know it yet, but she'd helped set off an epic rivalry that remains one of the most influential in the game's history.

"And there is Pat, outside the locker room, looking at the stats, angered face, and as I approach her, she looks up. And I said, 'This is going to be an unbelievable rating'—and it was, the highest rating ever for a women's college game—and she paused and said, 'For the good of the game.' And that was all she said."

Sports Illustrated

1995

UCLA DETHRONES ARKANSAS

CONNECTICUT
21

Perfect!

JENNIFER RIZZOTTI

PERFECT!

THE LAUNCH OF CONNECTICUT

Hi, it's Kate. OK, a personal story: I was fourteen years old in 1995, a freshman in high school, and already years into an obsession with basketball. One afternoon, the mail landed in the front hall of my childhood home—we had a slot to the right of our door—and I popped up from the couch to collect that day's bounty. There, facing upward, was that week's *Sports Illustrated*, and I stared down for a very long time. I couldn't believe what I was seeing.

I squatted to collect the magazine, then held it carefully in my hands: a women's basketball player was on the cover. And not just any women's basketball player, a college point guard named Jennifer Rizzotti, wearing kneepads and staring intently at the basketball, which was just on the edge of the frame. A single word cut across in orange letters: "Perfect!"

Beneath it, in white, it read, "Jennifer Rizzotti Propels Unbeaten Connecticut to the National Championship."

From the kitchen, I could hear my mom at the sink doing dishes, and I darted into the room and presented the magazine to her. She looked over, took it all in, and smiled.

"Wow, Kate, that's amazing!" she said.

And it was amazing. For so many reasons. First, that the University of Connecticut had gone unbeaten, 35–0, twice defeating legendary Tennessee, to win the program's first-ever national title. Second, that *Sports Illustrated*—at the time, the most important sports media real estate in the country—had decided to put the women's champion on the cover. And finally, that it was a point guard, and an action shot. Until that moment, I didn't realize how big my dreams could be.

But the world had answered: as big as you can imagine.

That 1994–95 season, Rizzotti was a junior. She was a local Connecticut kid who head coach Geno Auriemma had convinced, a few years prior, to come to UConn. UConn was going places, he told her. And he had a vision for how to get there. "It wasn't like UConn was the destination of choice by any means for players growing up, let alone kids from Connecticut," said Rizzotti, who is now president of the WNBA's Connecticut Sun. "Years later, everyone would always say, 'Oh that's so nice, you must have dreamed about playing there,' and I'm like, 'Actually no, they weren't covered, they weren't on TV yet. They weren't really a big thing.' Eventually, Geno sold me on attending there and my freshman year, we had a couple thousand fans at a game, sophomore year maybe five thousand a game, then by my junior year, which was that undefeated season, we started to sell out every game and we became a phenomenon."

Phenomenon is right. Connecticut's star player was Rebecca Lobo, a center, who would go on to play for the US Olympic team the following season. In fact, it was Lobo who told Rizzotti that a picture of her was going to be on the cover of *Sports Illustrated*. "We didn't have cell phones back then, so somehow she was on the phone and found out that we were going to be on the cover. And then, I was like, 'Oh my God, that's so awesome,' then she said it was going to be a picture of me and I was like, 'Whaaaat.' So we didn't know; it all came as a surprise. I think we found out just before it was coming out, but it was a pretty big moment."

UConn's run to the title, and the unprecedented media exposure that came with it, was a landmark moment. But, of course, the team would only understand this historical perspective later. "It's amazing to look back now and be like, that was the beginning of this ridiculous rivalry in women's basketball between us and Tennessee that helped catapult us, along with the '96 Olympic team, it helped catapult women's basketball to a whole other level in the United States. But in that year, and in that moment, none of us ever thought that was going to be the case."

Does Rizzotti now understand the cultural importance of that *Sports Illustrated* cover?

"Well, I still get it in the mail," she said. "To get autographed. I get it literally, probably, once or twice a month? Seriously. And now that I'm in Connecticut, I've gotten a bunch in the mail. 'Hey, can you autograph my *Sports Illustrated*?' It's amazing to me how many are out there unsigned, because I feel like I've signed every single copy of that *Sports Illustrated*."

UCONN TIMELINE DATA

"The Birth of a Dynasty"

★ First season (1974–75)

★ Hired Geno Auriemma (1985)

★ First-ever NCAA tournament appearance (1988–89)

★ First-ever Final Four (1990–91)

★ Lands biggest recruit in its history, Rebecca Lobo (1991)

★ First-ever undefeated season and NCAA title (1994–95)

★ First-ever matchup against Tennessee (1994–95)

AIR SWOOPES

THE STORY OF NIKE'S FIRST SIGNATURE SHOE

In 1993, Sheryl Swoopes exploded across the basketball world like a meteor, scoring forty-seven points in that year's NCAA title game, leading Texas Tech to its first, and only, national championship, and searing in everyone's consciousness the name—*Swoopes*—that would soon be emblazoned on sneakers around the world.

But before we get to the kicks, and the creation of them, let's explain why—why the moment was right for the first-ever women's signature shoe at Nike. Although Title IX had passed more than twenty years prior, Swoopes was part of the first generation of young athletes who could stand on the foundation built during those initial two decades. From this elevated platform, and for the first time, players could finally catch a beam of sunlight. Plus, the creation of the WNBA was just around the corner. In fact, soon after her stunning victory in the NCAA tournament, Swoopes was tapped to play for Team USA, which was hyperfocused on reclaiming gold at the upcoming 1996 Atlanta Olympics.

Nike saw opportunity. Swoopes was a player unlike any previously seen, with a last name to match her swagger and speed, and she was stepping onto the stage just as millions of eyes were turning toward women's basketball. The sports apparel behemoth, creators of the Air Jordan and other legendary silhouettes, tapped senior designer Marni Gerber to work with Swoopes to make the first-ever Air Swoopes. "I remember having lots of meetings," Gerber said of those initial days on the Nike campus. "Even at the beginning, it was whether we were going to call it the Air Swoopes because when someone's name is on a shoe, they get percentages, so it's a big business decision. It was exciting; it was definitely special. I was excited to work with an athlete, period. Because I always say, when you work with an athlete, the shoe designs itself."

Gerber first watched Swoopes play on video. Then she flew down to Lubbock, Texas—home of Texas Tech—to meet and talk with

Sheryl, to get a sense of who she was and what she wanted out of a sneaker.

At the time—and to this day, really—most women wore sneakers designed and built for men. And those sneakers tended to be overbuilt, and bulky, because that was the style that fit men better. (Kobe Bryant was actually one of the first male athletes to covet a lighter, underbuilt, sneaker.) "Unfortunately, I never got an opportunity to watch women play on TV growing up," Swoopes told *The Undefeated*. "I didn't know women could do this. So, I watched Michael Jordan. Anytime the Bulls were playing. I had to find a way to get in front of the TV.

I tried to take things from his game, emulate them, and put those into my game. He became my role model."

After meeting Swoopes, Gerber wanted a sneaker that would reflect the star's personality: sweet and soft-spoken off the court, but vicious and tenacious on it. She wanted to capture that contrast, while also designing a sneaker that cut back on the bulk. Swoopes also had requests: she wanted a middle strap, to help her feel secure in the sneaker, and she wanted great traction. On her visit, Gerber had joined the hooper on a trip to the hairdresser, and so for a personal touch—an Easter egg, of sorts—she chose a material with a linear pattern—an ode to the cornrows Swoopes occasionally wore.

"And the double 'S' on the bottom shows that kind of Sheryl Swoopes in-your-face when she's up in the air, flying through the air," Gerber said. "That was kind of a fun detail on the bottom. And then even the tongue-top logo, a graphic designer did that. It was a little bit more feminine. It was trying to do that feminine and tough both on the shoe."

Once the team at Nike had created a prototype, incorporating all of Swoopes's ideas, Gerber flew with the sneaker to Colorado Springs, where the future Olympian was training with Team USA. Gerber remembers Swoopes loving the prototype. "So, whatever we revised was probably more physical, if

anything—the strap was too short, or it was in the wrong place, so we tweaked things based on her foot."

On March 29, 1995, Nike announced the Air Swoopes at a press conference in New York City. It had been a decade since the company had named a shoe after an athlete, when it announced the Air Jordan in 1985. Pretty big footsteps to be following. At the event, Nike vice president of marketing Liz Dolan explained to gathered reporters why Nike was making the Air Swoopes. "One in three high school girls play sports," Dolan said. "But most women basketball players have bought men's shoes believing they're better. It's not true, but people have that feeling. So we needed to make a women's basketball shoe to make sure they're viewed as equal."

The original Air Swoopes, and all the subsequent versions, were only made in women's sizes, which limited the market—and potential commercial success—of the sneaker. Even if men wanted to buy the Swoopes, and many certainly did, the sneaker possessed a narrower design. Women can fit into men's sneakers because, if anything, they are simply wider. The reverse is not necessarily true. "In those days, and still today I think, women's product didn't get as much air time," Gerber said. "Men's shoes all get the glory of women being able to buy it, because they can fit in their shoes, but the women's shoes didn't get the numbers from the men because they couldn't fit into them."

Nike made seven iterations of the Air Swoopes, discontinuing the product in 2002—twenty years ago. As of 2022, Nike hasn't introduced another signature shoe for women's basketball into the market. "By the time Sheryl's shoe came out, I was too big to shop in the Lady Foot Locker and I couldn't get them," former WNBA star Seimone Augustus said, remembering the late nineties. "I assumed they would make shoes for the basketball player—we're obviously taller, bigger than the average woman. I was super bummed out because it was the first women's shoe to come out, and I wasn't able to get it. And I'm a hooper! And I love Sheryl Swooopes!"

HALFTIME SPEECH

L et us pause for a moment. We have reached the middle of this book, but hopefully we've just reached the beginning—or another inflection point—for the game. And while *Hoop Muses* is not meant for those who don't already love basketball, perhaps it's worth pulling away from our timeline of cool moments and history and lore and focusing for a minute on something less tangible: the invisible forces that have (sometimes unknowingly) shaped our beliefs about the game—its value, its place in the culture and in the economic pecking order.

In fact, let's start here: my house, the year is 2021, a good friend has come over for dinner, and the conversation has turned toward women's basketball.

This friend was a Division I athlete, and he asked me, tentatively, if he could explain why he doesn't watch women's sports. "Of course," I said, "let's hear it." I wanted nothing more than to understand why someone like him—a high-level athlete, a self-proclaimed feminist—had never turned on a women's basketball game. Or, more precisely, I wanted to hear why *he believes* he hasn't.

"I've actually thought about this a lot over the years," he said. "Because I often feel some level of guilt about it, but I think when it comes down to it, I just think that if I'm going to take the time to watch sports, I want to be watching them at the peak of how they can be played—speed, strength, all of it. And to me, that pinnacle is happening on the men's side."

I nodded as my friend spoke. He hit all the expected notes. *I don't watch because they can't dunk; I don't watch because they're like a good boys' high school team; I don't watch because, you know, I could probably beat them one-on-one.*

At its heart, this reasoning insists that people don't watch the WNBA because men run faster and jump higher. That is, in fact, true. Most men do run faster and jump higher. And, yes, it's incredibly exciting when one of those men runs fast and jumps high, and we watch, in awe, because we know for certain that he might be the only human capable of that particular feat.

It's a soothing rationale, this little story we tell ourselves about our insatiable appetite for windmill jams. It's foolproof, too, because this reasoning doesn't just absolve sports fans of any further introspection, but more importantly it absolves the marketers, the TV networks, and the sports apparel companies. Hell, it even seems to pardon the women themselves: *it's not your fault; sports fans crave something you just can't give them.* This reasoning, it presents itself as more than logical, it's...*biological.*

Actually, it's pathological. It's chronic, and irrational—stick around, I'll explain why—and it's stalked the WNBA since its founding. In the United States, this lie is the serial killer of women's professional leagues. (To name a few: the American Basketball League [1996–98], the Women's United Soccer Association [2000–03], the Women's Professional Softball League [1997–2001], and Women's Professional Soccer [2007–2012].)

The WNBA, though, is resilient. When launched in 1996, the league was ahead of its time—in almost every way. Long before big business saw the cultural value, the players of the W stood against racial injustice, and for equality, and took the hits—"Every direction we turned, we were walking into a wall," said WNBA legend Sue Bird—for representing the folks at society's margins. "People think you're supposed to look and talk and be a certain way, but the WNBA blasts all of those things out of the water," said A'ja Wilson of the Las Vegas Aces, the reigning league MVP. "And you should *want* that. We are standing on the shoulders of women who didn't back down just because casual sports fans didn't think they were worthy. That's what makes our league better, because we have faced those hurdles. I can't think of another league

EVERY
DIRECTION WE
TURNED, WE
WERE WALKING
INTO A WALL.
—SUE BIRD

that gets hit with every single last knock, and I don't see that going away, but we're not going to let that stop us."

Understanding why we watch sports isn't just a thought experiment. It has practical implications. Rather than passively believing the WNBA is biologically inferior, we can actively recognize that no athletes in modern history have faced more cultural obstacles than the players of the W. Not only are comparisons to the men ubiquitous—and the differences rendered clearer because of the unique intimacy of the sport—but, more important, no women's league has a higher percentage of Black athletes, meaning that for nearly a quarter century the WNBA has been rowing against the headwinds of racism, sexism, and homophobia.

Here we are, having celebrated the WNBA's twenty-fifth anniversary, and society's margins have reconfigured themselves, and today everyone inside the league feels similarly: that the world has finally caught up, that a movement has met its moment. In 2020, the league saw all meaningful metrics—social media impressions, TV ratings (up 68 percent), merchandise sales—skyrocket during its bubble season, which was just months after the players' union signed a new collective bargaining agreement that doesn't just raise salaries but encourages player movement, the fuel for year-round relevancy.

You might be wondering why, on the eve of the aforementioned birthday, I'm not taking you on a trip down memory lane, opening all the historical doors, peering into long-ago memories, maybe spinning an orange-and-oatmeal ball as we backpedal to 1996. The league, its foothold and its future, has never been guaranteed, so why not simply celebrate a milestone reached?

Because I think sports fans are ready for more context, more critical thinking about what drives their interest, as well as a league's growth. It's time. That aforementioned exchange, the one from my kitchen? It's not an anomaly. Some version of that exchange has played out millions of times—in cars and bars and coffee shops, among people of all genders and ages, in every year of the league's existence.

A quarter century ago, a group of stakeholders—former NBA commissioner David Stern leading them—believed the media exposure from a successful 1996 Summer Olympics in Atlanta could serve as a springboard for the larger goal of launching a newly formed professional basketball league, the WNBA, behind the backing of the NBA. From nothing to something, it was an inflection point for the game unlike any seen before, or since.

Until now. The promise of this second inflection point for the WNBA is to go from subsisting to thriving. The league has finally captured a slice of cultural relevancy, and if you're just casually paying attention, you might believe the outcome—this potential leveling up—will be solely determined by the players of the WNBA. You might believe some line about quality of play, etc.

But you'd be wrong. Here, I'll give Sue Bird the floor: "The story of twenty-five years, for a lot of people, the headline is: *Oh, they wouldn't exist if the NBA didn't keep them afloat; look how poorly they're doing.* But that's not the storyline. It's actually, look at corporate sponsorships, look at the media: *You didn't invest, you didn't do shit, and we're not just still here, we're actually growing.*"

The simple fact that in the last two decades Diana Taurasi has not blossomed into a transcendent mega-star is evidence enough that our sports world is not a meritocracy, as many pretend to believe. Anyone who's watched Taurasi play—or walk onto the court, or sit on the sidelines, or be anywhere, really—knows that she's impossible to look away from. Your eyes follow her, whether she has the ball or not. She's won four Olympic gold medals with Team USA and three WNBA titles with the Phoenix Mercury, and her popularity (outside of Phoenix) probably peaked in 2004, while playing in college for UConn. "I don't know if there's a bigger marketing ball that's been dropped than us not talking about Diana Taurasi nonstop," said former WNBA player and longtime ESPN analyst Rebecca Lobo. "Her name should have been like Serena Williams. It's not that great players haven't existed in the league; it's that we haven't done right by them. Taurasi should have been on national TV every week, and we should have been talking about her across the network."

Lobo is getting to the heart of the matter. The heart of why we *really* watch. What drives our interest in sports, generally speaking, are stakes and storylines. The stakes cannot be artificially constructed; they must be culturally agreed upon. Winning this game, this trophy, this tournament *matters*, in some larger sense. An incomplete list of the competitions we've agreed have significance: a title in any of the major sports (men's, of course), an NCAA title, the Grand Slam tennis tournaments, the Olympics, the World Cup. Regardless of the discipline, we'll passionately watch any Olympic event. We'll watch curling, and we'll care, because an Olympic gold medal is at stake and we are patriotic.

There are other events on the "matters" list, but a WNBA title is not yet there. It is for some fans, of course, but it's not yet hit a widespread cultural tipping point.

Go ahead and test this stakes-and-storyline theory. Imagine watching two lousy basketball players in a game of H-O-R-S-E. Yawn, right? Now imagine Mark Cuban walks by and announces that he'll give whoever wins a million dollars. Those are some agreed-upon stakes. Pull up a chair, get the popcorn ready. You might even start to feel your heart pounding, and you don't know these people. And they're not even good! (A baseball version of this happens in the series premiere of HBO's *Succession*.) Now imagine you do know one of the players. Imagine one of the shooters is your wife. Imagine if she wins this game, you know she'll finally be able to pay off her college loan debt and start that business she's always dreamed of. Bingo: stakes *and* storyline.

If, as fans, we agree upon the stakes and know at least one storyline, any game will thrill us. Your kid's high school match, riveting; the Little League World Series, a thing of beauty; the winter biathlon, can't-miss prime-time viewing. Just existing in our culture, we absorb, almost through osmosis, half a dozen NBA storylines. In Pixar's recent animated movie *Soul*, there's a joke built around the perennial ineptitude of the New York Knicks. Hell, Apple TV will literally interrupt whatever show you're streaming to alert you that a game is close. Men's sports will invade our personal space, often without permission, so that one day when you're flipping through the channels and you see the Lakers playing the Knicks, you almost certainly know a few storylines. (*Oh, yeah, Lebron's in Los Angeles...*) You might stop and watch a couple minutes, and probably not because some proficient skill thrilled you.

IT'S NOT THAT GREAT PLAYERS HAVEN'T EXISTED IN THE LEAGUE; IT'S THAT WE HAVEN'T DONE RIGHT BY THEM. TAURASI SHOULD HAVE BEEN ON NATIONAL TV EVERY WEEK, AND WE SHOULD HAVE BEEN TALKING ABOUT HER ACROSS THE NETWORK.
—REBECCA LOBO

The WNBA might stand a fighting chance if, just existing in our culture, the message we absorbed about the league was neutral, or even nonexistent. But it's not. The league isn't even afforded the common courtesy of apathy, which would allow curious prospective fans to make up their own minds. Instead, the W is the butt of lame jokes during comedy specials and poorly written *Saturday Night Live* skits and aggressive trolling on social media. In this culture, when you're not even seeking it out, people will invade your space to tell you how *lame* the WNBA is—*that's* the storyline absorbed through osmosis. So, in this way, the culture ties the laces of the W, forcing them to battle just to reach the starting line, just to remove the poison from their water.

"When I hear the argument of 'quality of play' or shooting percentages—or points scored, or whatever—as reasons people don't watch, those are all just excuses to continue pointing to the players, to the women, as scapegoats," said Nneka Ogwumike, former league MVP and president of the players' union. "When do we look elsewhere? As a Black woman in this country, I know my magic and value and worth. So, what about the accountability of the business to do the business?"

Every square inch of the NBA has been, or is currently being, exploited—physically,

I'M NOT IN THE TV BUSINESS, BUT I FEEL LIKE IT'S NOT THAT HARD TO PUT US ON TV. IT'S AN EFFORT THING.—JEWELL LOYD

digitally, and financially. Innovators offering even the slightest advantages—some small data insight, juicing beets for better oxygen absorption, creating secondary revenue streams by selling game-worn uniforms—are rewarded with Wall Street–level salaries. Where there is cash, talent follows. So, in a world like this, what is the WNBA but, at best, a stepping stone? Generally speaking, if someone is good at their job in the W, they move on; and if they're not, they stay. The NBA is the best 450 players in the world, surrounded by the best marketers, merchandisers, communications directors, salespeople, trainers, and analysts. With few exceptions, the same cannot be said for the W, except for the part about the players—they're the best 144 in the world.

Armed with all that information, fans can continue believing the WNBA flies below the radar because they don't fly above the rim. Or fans can glance at the infrastructure of the sports world—i.e., the programming decisions made by ESPN, the marketing dollars budgeted by Nike, the cover (and *coverage*) decisions of magazines—and wonder if perhaps, maybe, women aren't invested in the same way men are. "There is a direct correlation: if something is supported—monetarily, or in love, or in going the extra mile—then success is going to happen," said Dawn Staley, former WNBA star and current University of South Carolina head coach. "If we pour into the W what they

poured into the NBA from year twenty-five to fifty, we'll have a team in every city and we'll fly charter, and we'll have sneaker contracts that are multi-million deals."

During the pandemic season of 2020, ESPN more than doubled its slate of regular season WNBA games, airing thirty-seven, up from just sixteen the previous season. (The network was desperate for live programming.) It was the kind of dream experiment that many women's sports advocates had long called for. It was the old Field of Dreams argument: *If you build it, they will come.* People had been saying for years that more airtime would drive better ratings, would justify more airtime, would drive even better ratings. "A huge thing for us is breadth of coverage," said WNBA commissioner Cathy Engelbart. "That ratings increase was because we had more games on and people would say, 'Oh, it's just because you had more games on'—as if we didn't earn it. And I said, 'Well, isn't that the point?'"

"I'm not in the TV business," said two-time WNBA champion Jewell Loyd of the Seattle Storm, "but I feel like it's not that hard to put us on TV. It's an effort thing."

You know that Aristotle quote, "The whole is greater than the sum of its parts"? Somehow, when it comes to the first twenty-five years of the WNBA, the whole has been less than the sum of its parts. That is to say, all of the league's tangential stakeholders, the Nikes and the ESPNs, profess dedication to the growth of the game. All of the outward noises from such companies tell the story of sport as universal, of game recognizing game. The bird's-eye view shows companies trading on equality; yet their day-to-day decisions rarely live up to those lofty ideals. Nike hasn't introduced a new signature women's basketball shoe in twenty-five years, since Sheryl Swoopes debuted the Air Swoopes in 1996. ESPN pays $12 million a year for the right to broadcast the WNBA, then routinely airs only a fraction of the games, burying the league on its less-watched channels and deep on its website, and offering almost no studio programming to generate storylines and interest. "My wish is that ESPN would drive the push for the WNBA instead of waiting," said Lobo. "I wish we would drive the conversation. The WNBA has gotten cool, and ESPN needs to understand that it's a cool thing."

(If you're doubting the WNBA's growing cool factor, especially among the younger demographic, you're probably looking in the wrong places. The evidence exists on social—Instagram, Snapchat, TikTok—where Images of the players' 'fits [i.e., out*fits*] as they walk into the arena get tagged and linked and reshared. In this way, players of the W are burgeoning fashion icons. "We were once seen as outsiders," said Bird, who this winter was on the cover of *GQ* with her fiancée, soccer star Megan Rapinoe. "But society caught up with us.")

The latest study analyzing sports media coverage shows, once again, that female athletes receive about 2 percent of airtime on ESPN's *SportsCenter*—about the same as it's been for decades. Cue the chicken-and-the-egg: is the WNBA given little coverage because people don't want it, or do people not want it because it's given little coverage?

"People in every other industry understand that demand is created by the marketers and the decision-makers," said Nefertiti Walker, professor of sport business at the University of Massachusetts Amherst. "They know: people watch what you tell them to watch, what you create bells and whistles around them watching. Only sports people, when making decisions about investing in women, throw up their hands and act like the consumers drive decisions."

The crazy thing is that even that 2 percent—that tiny, little number—actually overstates the coverage given women. Because that 2 percent is almost always either a highlight or an anomaly (e.g., the much-publicized on-court fight involving the Detroit Shock in 2008). It's a one-off. It's almost never a storyline, which offers continuity, which often sparks debate, which has elements of inheritance, passed down from one generation to the next. Inheritance in sports isn't talked about enough. The only women's team sport that is on the cusp of generational inheritance is the US women's national soccer team. Almost certainly, any player who wears that uniform in the future will find awaiting them a rabid fan base, an elevated platform—something like stardom. But the USWNT has, among other advantages, the racial makeup of its talent pool—predominantly white—and the rare double-double of the Olympics and World Cup, two stakes-and-storylines events. (Yes, the WNBA also has the Olympics, but the team usually toils in the shadow of that year's iteration of *the* Dream Team, the men.)

On the other hand, most male athletes grow up knowing that if they excel, a kingdom awaits. The best NBA player will always transcend his game, because his sport includes an altar at which we all worship. It also includes inherited storylines, which fuel media coverage, and will always exist regardless of the specific personnel in the league.

"We're never a talking point," said Bird. "If we're covered, it's a highlight. And there are times when some of those anchors, they know their shit, and you can tell. And there are times when they're just reading copy. But either way, we are never a storyline topic: *Should this coach be fired? Should that player be traded? This player is on the max contract, why?* We never have talking heads talking about us."

I spent seven years at ESPN and routinely pitched WNBA topics during morning production meetings. Resistance existed because "the guys don't know much about the WNBA" and it "wouldn't make for good TV." Well, we could have said the same about every NHL topic we introduced, but the assumption was that people would get educated. That was the job. Yet somehow that logic didn't extend to the WNBA. And once, when we finally tried a segment, it did, in fact, fall flat. Nobody had done their homework. My male colleagues couldn't name more than one player. The verdict was, "See, that didn't work; the WNBA isn't compelling."

The players in the W, as is often the case, identified the problem, and worked to introduce a fix—themselves. As the 2020 deadline for a new collective bargaining agreement approached, the players knew that a lot of foundational issues needed reworking—issues going back to the beginning. When the league launched, they essentially just borrowed all the wisdom from the NBA. Whatever the NBA did, the W just followed the blueprint. Those first years, the power resided at the league level, for big things, like deciding which players would play in what cities (Lisa Leslie to Los Angeles; Cynthia Cooper to Houston, etc.), to the small things, like how players should be marketed, how they should look in a photo shoot (i.e., "straight"). "In the beginning, the league was trying to have players fit the image they weren't," said reigning WNBA Finals MVP Breanna Stewart. "And it was because the league thought that's what was best for the league. I remember Sue and [Taurasi] telling me: 'If you don't feel comfortable doing a photo shoot, don't do it.' There are pictures of them wearing things that they wouldn't wear. Back then, they weren't able to be the exact person they are. But that's changed."

It's one of many gradual changes that the WNBA has integrated on the fly, while still playing, while still fighting for their future. In many ways, the league is a completely different specimen than when it launched. Like the story of the ship of Theseus, which asks if an object remains fundamentally the same if all its parts have been replaced, the WNBA has been in a steady state of renovation, one piece at a time. Many casual fans think they know what the league is, because maybe they checked it out once at the beginning, or maybe a friend of theirs made some snide comment. But it's nothing like it was. Over the last quarter century, the power has migrated from the league, to the teams, and finally, now, to the players—where it has always belonged.

The collective bargaining agreement signed in 2020 is an agreement with an eye to the future. Some of the more important aspects are obvious. The players fought for changes that allowed for more player movement, which they rightly recognized as the lifeblood of off-season coverage. A player now reaches free agency after five years, not six, and the number of times a team can "core" a player—similar to the NFL's franchise tag—drops from four

to three, and a year later, down to two. Right away, Candace Parker left Los Angeles for Chicago—a splashy move almost impossible under the old agreement. And now we have a new storyline: the blossoming of a rivalry.

But there are additional shades within the agreement that highlight the players' keen understanding of why people watch sports. Take, for example, the new maximum contract of $500,000, more than triple the previous number. They know that only a few players can achieve that salary, but that wasn't the point at all: the headline was the point. The point was to break free of the flawed narrative that WNBA players don't make money. You know what doesn't sell tickets? The belief that female players make less money than schoolteachers. The NBA, NFL, MLB lifestyle is an aspirational lifestyle. Not just the athleticism, but also the money, the culture, the fashion, the cachet—it all adds up to cultural capital.

Watching sports is communal, even when alone. It's about being a part of something— often first with your family, growing up, then with your community, whether a high school, a college, or a city. You'll often hear the argument that if women aren't watching women's sports, then men shouldn't be bothered to care, either. But that's irrational, because women watch sports for mostly the same reasons men do. "There's a certain cultural value, status and inclusion that you get as a sports fan if you're a fan of men's sports," said Cheryl Cooky, professor at Purdue University and author of *No Slam Dunk: Gender, Sport and the Unevenness of Social Change*. "Men's sports transcend sports itself and becomes a part of the larger cultural consciousness. Of course, both women and men want to be a part of that cultural conversation."

People watch sports because of how it makes them feel. Sometimes that feeling is nostalgic or tense or blissful, but more often the feeling is cool—they want to feel *cool*. It's why courtside seats for the aforementioned New York Knicks, with only three winning seasons this century and even fewer bona fide stars, still sell for thousands of dollars, and why,

during the games, the Madison Square Garden staff plays the latest hip-hop even though its most expensive seats are filled by forty- and fifty-year-olds, because those guys don't want to hear what's on their stale Spotify playlists; they want to live inside a moment where they're ageless and timeless, part of what's young and relevant.

The opposite of cool is a cause. And too often throughout the years, the pitch for the WNBA has been something like: *supporting it is the right thing to do—for our daughters*. Even though the top players stockpile cash overseas alongside their W contracts, and alongside separate apparel and marketing deals, and even

IF WE POUR INTO THE W WHAT THEY POURED INTO THE NBA FROM YEAR TWENTY-FIVE TO FIFTY, WE'LL HAVE A TEAM IN EVERY CITY AND WE'LL FLY CHARTER, AND WE'LL HAVE SNEAKER CONTRACTS THAT ARE MULTI-MILLION DEALS.
—DAWN STALEY

PEOPLE WATCH SPORTS BECAUSE OF HOW IT MAKES THEM FEEL.

though most of the top players have multiple homes and numerous investments, the general belief exists that they don't make *lifestyle* money. And that perpetuates the idea of the W as a kind of charity, as a kind of Title IX offshoot. Maybe that was true during the 2000s, but it's not anymore. Investors are just beginning to recognize the tremendous long-term value in owning a WNBA franchise.

Look no further than Mark Davis's recent acquisition of the Las Vegas Aces. Said Lobo: "Every time a WNBA team has gotten a new owner it's like, 'Do they have money, or do they have reaaaaaal money?' Because on the NBA side, people have *real* money. You need owners with money-money, owners who say, 'This is a status thing for me. I'm proud to sit courtside and wear their gear.'"

The W has rarely had owners with Bill Gates–type money—you know, yacht money, spend-too-much-on-a-role-player-cause-I-wanna-win money. "Mark clearly has a passion for the WNBA and he's clearly seen that there's growth potential," said Engelbart. "His purchase is a great sign for us. Mark wouldn't be here if he didn't clearly see growth potential. Investors are now kind of saying, 'Hmmm, yeah, this is pretty interesting to me.'"

When Art Rooney founded the Pittsburgh Steelers in 1933, something like 90 percent of NFL franchises had failed. The modern-day NBA claims that half of its franchises lose money. Entering the 2020 COVID-affected NBA season, one executive said all thirty teams would lose money. This is not to say everyone believes NBA owners when they cry poor, but rather that a specific team's profit and loss sheet has never been used to degrade the athletes themselves. If you're still concerned about the W's profit and loss statements, consider that the combined salary of the league's 144 players is about $15 million, which means that more than eighty individual players in the NBA make more in one season than all W players combined, and which means also that most NBA teams are spending more money paying the contracts of players who aren't even currently in the league than the entirety of what the WNBA makes or loses. "Historically, owners of men's teams have had a very different attitude," said Dave Barry, professor of economics at Southern Utah University. "They've cared less about gate receipts and more about winning and losing and *love of the game*. It's often a vanity project—just to be involved in the game. But suddenly when it's women's sports, you have to make a profit; now you're running a McDonald's? Now we have to pore over profit and loss statements? And it's like, when did we decide that's how we evaluate things in sports? The takeaway is that we love investing in men. Wow, do we ever."

If you listen to what Mark Davis is saying, he's planning on *investing* because he sees *potential*. That may seem like common sense, but for female athletes it's revolutionary. Male athletes are paid based on their potential, then invested in so they reach it, and it sounds very much like that's what Davis has in mind for the Aces. A new 50,000-square-foot practice facility near the Raiders, perhaps an arena all their own—all this after a sit-down conversation with the team's star, Wilson, to get her buy-in. "Players on marquees on the strip, flying first class to All-Star; we set a bar that's so high," Wilson said of the Aces. "And we look at other teams and we might not have championships yet, but we are setting another kind of bar."

"We're here to push the envelope," said Loyd. "Our generation, we're like, *fuck it, we're gonna do it*. A little bit of me is saying coaches aren't coaches unless there are players; a league isn't a league unless there are players. We aren't asking for a Lambo and a penthouse suite. We aren't asking for crazy things. But this generation is fearless. That's how we play

and that's how we feel about the future. And it's like, *get on board*."

Everyone around the game knows that over the last few seasons the ground has shifted beneath them; they just don't know how to react. So the question isn't if anyone will heed Loyd's directive, but rather who will be next and how soon. Will it be ESPN, reevaluating its lukewarm commitment to the W and doubling its on-air presence? Or will it be Nike (or Puma, or Reebok, or Under Armour) finally accepting culpability—that they've been like vampires: marketing the abstract concept of *female power*, and of sport as equal, while contributing to its inequality? Or perhaps it will be some blue-chip company recognizing it can partner with women, and predominantly Black women, and benefit from a quarter century of the league's blood, sweat, and tears? Whoever moves first will benefit most.

Yeah, Taurasi should have been the Jordan, but maybe, just like the league itself, she was ahead of her time. Maybe the Jordan is about to walk through the doors. And when that player does arrive, all the scales and models that say women's basketball players only get *this much*—*this much* airtime, salary, marketing dollars, investment—will be blown to smithereens. Because those models are already creaking under the weight of their absurdity, because those models were built without vision, meant to offer women a place but not a chance.

THE
GAME
CHANGERS

AN ICONIC
SPORTS ILLUSTRATED
COVER

The photographer, Lois Greenfield, was renowned in the dance world, and known for her ability to capture the grace and fluidity of movement. *Sports Illustrated* had tapped her before, for a spread on the Memphis Tigers men's team as part of its 1995–96 college basketball preview. The similarities between the two shoots are unmistakable, with players seemingly floating through space. "Some people like that static moment, but I have no interest in that," Greenfield said of her style. "I like something that's in process, that has some momentum to it."

1 This cover shoot wasn't done at Greenfield's studio, where there wouldn't have been enough space. Today, most photo shoots have real-time feedback monitors, but back then Greenfield just had her main camera and a Polaroid camera, which would show her (somewhat quickly) if everyone was making it into frame—if the general idea was working. Part of what Greenfield had going for her was that she wasn't bogged down with what the athlete's movements "should" look like. "I know nothing about basketball except you're supposed to make it in the basket," she said.

2 Greenfield believes this cover image is mostly one image she captured, perhaps a composite of two.

3 She took 190 shots total.

4 Sheryl Swoopes (jersey number 7) is wearing the Air Swoopes, which she debuted on Team USA's year-long tour leading up to the Atlanta Olympics.

5 Teresa Edwards (player far right) was the veteran of the '96 squad and the link connecting Team USA's first-ever gold medal in 1984 with this "Dream Team" iteration. Teresa Edwards played in five Olympics (winning four golds), a record until Sue Bird and Diana Taurasi captured their fifth gold medals at the 2020 Games.

6 Edwards and Katrina McClain (behind Ruthie Bolton, jersey number 6) were the only two members of the '96 team who'd been on the roster for the 1992 Barcelona Olympics, where Team USA had disappointed with only the bronze medal. It was this "failure" that sparked the different tactic by USA Basketball: a full-year tour ahead, time to gel, commitment to reclaiming gold.

8 Teresa Edwards was selected to read the athlete's oath at the opening ceremonies, so she spent the morning of the ceremony traveling around the city with President Bill Clinton and family. "I was just trying to keep up with him and not get in the Secret Service's way!" she said.

9 Lisa Leslie (jersey number 9) went on to be one of the three cornerstones of the WNBA's founding—along with Olympic teammates Rebecca Lobo (not shown) and Swoopes (jersey number 7). Leslie was a University of Southern California star; she played in four Olympics and was an eight-time WNBA all-star and two-time WNBA champion.

10 These five players comprised the team's Olympic starting lineup.

11 Six members of the 1996 team also represented the US in 2000: Sheryl Swoopes, Dawn Staley, Lisa Leslie, Teresa Edwards, Nikki McCray, and Ruthie Bolton.

YOU GO, GIRLS! 🔟
1️⃣1️⃣ The U.S. Women's Basketball Team

7 Coach Tara VanDerveer (far right) was captured in many different poses, often just jumping in the air; this "timeout call" pose seemed to capture her in a purposeful movement and ultimately made the most sense to the shot's composition. VanDerveer was an integral part of the making of this '96 team—she took a year off from Stanford to dedicate herself to reestablishing America's dominance on the world stage.

AND SO IT BEGINS

THE BACKSTORY ON THE WNBA'S LAUNCH

More than a decade before the inaugural season of the Women's National Basketball Association tipped off on June 21, 1997, way back in 1985, a twenty-seven-year-old Nancy Lieberman received a call from David Stern, then only a year into his twenty-year tenure as commissioner of the NBA.

"So, I fly to New York," Lieberman said. "And we go into his office in Manhattan, and he closes the door and, me being me, I go, 'Why are you closing the door?' and he looks at me and he goes, 'I don't want anybody to hear this.' And I said, 'Hear what?' and he goes, 'Nancy, before I'm done as commissioner of the NBA, there's going to be a Women's National Basketball Association.' I about dropped it right there in his office, and I said, 'What are you talking about?' And he said, 'There will be a W.'"

But at that point, the WNBA was just an idea—although one that existed inside the mind of, perhaps, the most important businessman in the game. Developing the league, bringing it to fruition, would still take another decade. And, actually, among the pivotal moments were a couple of painful losses.

It was the summer of 1992, and the world was abuzz with the men's Dream Team. You know the squad: Michael Jordan and Magic Johnson and Larry Bird—the team that won the gold medal in Barcelona by beating the next best team, Croatia, by *thirty-two points*. What you might not know is that, at those same Olympics, the US women's national basketball

team missed the gold medal game. Team USA was upset by the Unified Team (formerly the Soviet Union) in the semifinals, and the Americans settled for bronze.

And then two years later, at the World Championships, the women got bronze...again.

"Part of the reason we got the bronze was the team didn't practice very much," said Val Ackerman, then on the board of directors for USA Basketball, and eventually the first commissioner of the WNBA. "Women played overseas, then had a couple weeks of practice leading up. The idea that developed in advance of

IS THERE ANY WAY WE CAN CREATE A DREAM TEAM FOR THE WOMEN?

the 1996 Atlanta Olympics was 'Is there any way we can create a Dream Team for the women?'"

Stern had already started putting into motion the idea of the W, and in that moment, it became clear: use the '96 Olympics as the launching point. And to give the team the best chance of success, have them together for an entire year before the Olympics, touring the country and overseas.

"We worked up a budget and computed that it would cost $3 million—players and coaches—to tour for the year," Ackerman said. "We thought we could offset it with sponsorships. I would get phone calls from people telling us that we shouldn't do this, but David said, 'Tell USA basketball that we'll pay for it. The NBA is good if there is shortfall.'"

This wasn't goodwill. Well, it wasn't *entirely* goodwill. Because as Team USA toured in advance of Atlanta, the NBA put together an internal working group with the heads of each department—broadcasting, sponsorship, communication—with the goal of launching a women's professional league the year following the Olympics, in 1997. This new league, the WNBA, would run during the summer months, so that NBA owners would have basketball in their arenas year-round.

As Ackerman explained, during that 1995–96 season, with Team USA touring the country, the NBA's in-house brain trust was watching closely as a proof of concept, as a kind of real-life vision board.

Then came the 1996 Atlanta Olympics,

and the pressure on Team USA to win gold was enormous. Not just because it was the Olympics, which brings its own weight, but also because of what lay on the horizon: finally, a domestic pro league with the kind of financial backing to give the women's game a legitimate, fighting chance at professional survival. "For the NBA and owners, the sell was year-round ownership of basketball," Ackerman said. "We are going to create a women's league with the best players in the world. Our mantra was to become the fifth major league sport."

Of course, as has been well documented, Team USA gelled during their year-long tour, then absolutely dominated in Atlanta. In total, the group played sixty games. They won every single one: fifty-two in the lead-up to the games, and eight in the Olympics themselves, winning one of the most visible gold medals and establishing the USA as the dominant force it has remained for nearly three decades.

Back home in New York, the NBA had its ducks in a row. They had secured sponsorship deals with numerous founding partners—General Motors, Coca-Cola, Proctor & Gamble, to name a few—and landed on the eight cities (and teams) that would become charter franchises.

The NBA had the blueprint of how it had built the men's game, but in launching the W, it was setting out to achieve where many others had failed. "We knew going in this was going

THIS NEW LEAGUE, THE WNBA, WOULD RUN DURING THE SUMMER MONTHS, SO THAT NBA OWNERS WOULD HAVE BASKETBALL IN THEIR ARENAS YEAR-ROUND.

THERE will be a W

"WE GOT NEXT"

A Campaign That Launched a Vision

The phrase *We got next* is ubiquitous on the playground. All hoopers know it. It means a player has, quite literally, assembled a team, and that squad is ready to take on the winner of the game currently being played. The marketing gurus behind the launch of the WNBA decided to turn this idea into the league's first-ever slogan. And on April 24, 1996, this vision was unveiled in a thirty-second spot on NBC. The ad begins with three fierce women—Lisa Leslie in front, Rebecca Lobo and Sheryl Swoopes just behind—walking toward the camera. They are nineties chic: oversize leather jackets, a backward beret. Over their shoulders are slung blue bags and we zoom in: they're emblazoned with the WNBA logo, each player's last name in cursive above. The women exchange glances with one another. *Oh,* the *looks suggest, these women are ready* to *bring it.* The copy reads: "This Summer. We Got Next. Opening Tip. June 21, 1997."

WE ARE GOING TO CREATE A WOMEN'S LEAGUE WITH THE BEST PLAYERS IN THE WORLD.

to be a challenging endeavor because women's pro ball had not done well previously," said Ackerman. "The research showed us that there were fifteen or more attempts to start women's professional leagues that had all failed. Some had never gotten past the press conference. They were basically graveyards. We knew we had our work cut out for us, but we thought we were a different animal because of the NBA's backing, the summer season, this whole lining up of the stars that was different than what other leagues had."

They tried to innovate: the cream-and-orange-colored ball, the fabric of the uniforms, the summer season, the focus on storytelling. In August 1996, the WNBA announced itself to the world; a little less than a year later, the first-ever game, the New York Liberty versus the Los Angeles Sparks, tipped off with more than 10,000 fans in attendance.

THE
RIVALRY

THE ABL TIMES IT JUST WRONG

One brief moment inside a Palo Alto mall helped launch one of the most ambitious professional leagues ever created: the American Basketball League (ABL). The year was 1995 and, as Maitreyi Anantharaman writes in Defector, it was the day that NBA star Chris Webber had just signed his first NBA contract, worth millions. A woman named Anne Cribbs, who worked in public relations, was at the mall with her daughter looking in a sporting goods store for a pair of socks. As she checked out, she recognized the young woman behind the register: former Stanford basketball star Molly Goodenbour.

Goodenbour was a two-time national champion, and in 1992 was named NCAA tournament Most Outstanding Player in leading the Cardinal to the title. Cribbs was disheartened at the sight of the talented Goodenbour, presumably making minimum wage, while her male counterpart (the aforementioned Webber) was being launched into a different stratosphere.

Cribbs and business partner Gary Cavalli worked with Stanford Athletics, so they were intimately familiar with the dominance of Tara VanDerveer's program, as well as how much energy could surround the game when properly built. The two kidded about starting a women's professional league. Of course, they didn't have the money for something like that.

But Steve Hams, an executive in Silicon Valley, did. And he'd been cooking up a business plan to launch a league. (Like Cribbs and Cavalli, Hams was a fan of Stanford's legendary women's teams.) Soon, the trio connected and started turning the daydream into a reality.

They knew they had a few things going for them, most notably the upcoming 1996 Atlanta Olympics, during which women's basketball promised to be a showcase event.

They studied the past failures of professional leagues, hoping to learn from history. They wanted to build a league that fostered trust and respect with the players, paying them a true living wage and benefits, even giving them a voice in how things were done. They also seized on a key insight: that professional women's teams didn't need to chase the biggest markets, but rather ones that had already shown a propensity toward supporting the women's game.

COLUMBUS QUEST FIRST TITLE

Nikki McCray
Katie Smith
Valerie Still
Pee Wee Johnson
Sonja Tate

Slowly, the group started recruiting the stars of the upcoming Olympic team. First up was Jennifer Azzi, former Stanford guard. At this point, in 1995, the WNBA did not yet exist—it was merely a rumor, as it had been for years. Azzi said yes. Soon after, Teresa Edwards came aboard. Then Dawn Staley. Pretty soon, they had commitments from most of the Olympic roster. "It's hard to describe how hopeful we were, even if this thing was just a packet of paper and Steve was some guy we didn't know," Azzi told author Sara Corbett, who wrote the book *Venus to the Hoop*, chronicling the '96 Olympic team.

Then, in April 1996, just a few months before the Olympics, NBA's vice president of affairs, Val Ackerman, held a press conference in New York and announced the WNBA, backed by the NBA, and scheduled to launch in the summer of 1997. By then, only three Olympic stars hadn't signed contracts with the ABL:

Sheryl Swoopes, Lisa Leslie, and UConn star Rebecca Lobo. The other nine were committed to the ABL.

The league pushed forward. The leadership had always known an NBA-backed league was a possibility; NBA commissioner David Stern had hinted as much for years. The ABL announced its eight founding franchises: the Atlanta Glory, Columbus Quest, Colorado Xplosion, San Jose Lasers, Seattle Reign, Richmond Rage, Portland Power, and the New England Blizzard. And just a few months after Team USA captured the gold medal, the ABL's inaugural forty-game season began.

The WNBA's first season tipped off a few months after the Columbus Quest won the first-ever ABL title, three games to two, over Staley's Richmond Rage. Even though most fans agreed that the ABL's talent pool was deeper and quality of play stronger, the ABL couldn't match the WNBA's deep pockets and its TV network and sponsorship connections.

Cavalli attempted to link the ABL to the WNBA, first calling Ackerman about a joint

WHY WOULD WE PUT A W ON THERE? THEY DON'T PUT ONE ON THE MEN.

SYLVIA CRAWLEY

WNBA
$50K
↑
$15K

ABL
$100K
+ BENEFITS
↑
$40K

all-star game pitting each league's best players against one another. Ackerman declined. Soon, the WNBA was signing ABL players whose one-year deals had expired. The glitz and glamour of the NBA spotlight proved difficult for the gritty ABL to overcome. As a last-ditch effort, Cavalli met Ackerman for lunch and pitched her on the idea of merging the two leagues. A few weeks later, in an email, Ackerman responded: *thanks, but no thanks*.

The ABL officially ceased operations about a dozen games into their third season. "We fought the good fight, and we had a good run," Cavalli wrote in a prepared statement in 1998. "But we were unable to obtain the television exposure and sponsorship support needed to make the league viable long-term."

★ The American Basketball League purposely omitted "women" from its title. "Why would we put a W on there? They don't put one on the men," said legend Sylvia Crawley at the time.

★ Columbus Quest wins first title with Nikki McCray, Katie Smith, Valerie Still, Pee Wee Johnson, Sonja Tate.

★ Columbus Quest won *both* ABL titles.

★ The ABL finals MVP won a Nissan Altima.

★ Four thousand six hundred people packed the San Jose State Events Center to watch the opening night ABL game between the Lasers and Glory, which featured Azzi on San Jose and Teresa Edwards on Atlanta.

★ Staffers for the ABL wore t-shirts that said, "100 percent."

★ In that first year, the ABL had more talent and was more about ball, whereas the WNBA leaned on Swoopes, Leslie, and Lobo, and Lisa Leslie saying things like, "I think it's important for girls to know that they don't have to look like boys to play like boys."

★ WNBA salary was $15,000 to $50,000 vs. ABL's $40,000 to $100,000 with year-round benefits.

SAN JOSE STATE EVENTS CENTER 1996 | 4600 PPL
LASERS vs GLORY

VAN AND THE COMETS

COOP, SWOOPES, AND TINA GO BACK-TO-BACK-TO-BACK-TO-BACK

Behind every dynasty is destiny. A stroke (or *strokes*) of good luck. Something a little like fate. Few athletes want to admit this—because blood, sweat, and tears are more tangible—but every so often things come together in just the right way, and a team meets its moment.

This is true of the Houston Comets, one of the eight original WNBA franchises. It's no small matter, creating a league and franchises from nothing, and one of the pressing concerns was assigning players to teams (and cities) for maximum impact. This had to be balanced against fairness: each franchise should start with approximately the same talent level, the same chance at competing in that first year.

And here's where fate first comes into play. In the decade before the WNBA's existence, Cynthia Cooper had been playing in Spain and Italy. Actually, she'd been dominating in those countries. Before that, she'd won back-to-back

titles at the University of Southern California with the legendary Cheryl Miller. For people in the know, Cooper was one of the best in the game, but she'd been toiling away in obscurity for years. She had fallen so off the radar that, two years prior, when Cooper heard about the formation of the American Basketball League, she called the office and pitched herself as a player. They passed. Too many guards, they told her.

"When I came to the WNBA, I knew that nobody knew what I was about," Cooper said. "There were a handful of people who knew because they had played against me overseas. But really nobody knew who I was as a player and what I'd been doing for years. So, I was a surprise, but I wasn't the biggest one."

Val Ackerman, the league's first commissioner, put it this way to ESPN's *The Undefeated*: "I think we blew it. None of us realized just how good Cynthia Cooper was, because if we had, she would not have been assigned to the Comets…If we had any inkling of how dominant a player she was, we would have…spread it. We just didn't know."

Five months before the first game, on January 22, 1997, Cooper was assigned to the Houston Comets along with one other player.

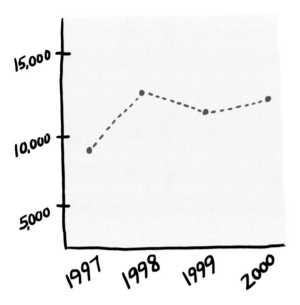

15,000
10,000
5,000

1997 1998 1999 2000

pick, Houston selected USC star Tina Thompson, who would go on to have a hall of fame career. Explained Cooper: "Before we stepped on the court, it was, 'Who is this Cynthia Cooper kid and who is Tina Thompson going to become as a professional player? How are they going to work together? Are there enough balls? How are their personalities going to mesh or not?'"

Whether by coincidence or by design, the Comets landed a coach known for blending the kinds of egos and personalities that peppered the Houston roster. His name was Van Chancellor. He'd been at Ole Miss for nineteen seasons before he said yes to jumping to the WNBA. "When I took that pro job, I felt like I was thirty years old again," he told the SEC

Now, who was that one other player? None other than Sheryl Swoopes, who made perfect sense for the Houston franchise. She was Texas born and raised and had exploded onto the scene while leading Texas Tech to the 1993 NCAA championship. At the outset of the WNBA, Swoopes was almost certainly the game's biggest star: she had a signature shoe with Nike, the Air Swoopes, and had just won gold with Team USA. Along with Lisa Leslie (Los Angeles) and Rebecca Lobo (New York), Swoopes was a league cornerstone.

Which is why (hello again, fate) the league felt it necessary to award the Comets the number one pick in the inaugural draft, to offset the fact that Swoopes was pregnant and scheduled to miss the entire opening season. (She returned just six weeks after giving birth.) With the top

Van Chancellor
MISSISSIPPI HOUSTON COMETS LSU

HIGHEST WINNING PERCENTAGE **Comets** IN HISTORY OF NBA AND WNBA

Network in 2015. "I was up at six in the morning almost every day, ready to roll. I knew that anytime you leave home on a new adventure, there's going to be a lot of uncertainties. But in my mind, it was either take that once-in-a-lifetime chance or sit and watch it go by. I took it and it rekindled my coaching career."

The rest is not just history, it's historic. The Comets, behind the Big Three (Swoopes, Cooper, Thompson), won the inaugural WNBA title, with Cooper being named league MVP. They'd win the second title, too, then the third, and, finally, the fourth. "I think we proved that we could come together and play when we had that common goal," Cooper said. "And that was to win a championship."

2008

★ The eight original W franchises: the Charlotte Sting, Cleveland Rockers, Houston Comets, and New York Liberty in the Eastern Conference; and the Los Angeles Sparks, Phoenix Mercury, Sacramento Monarchs, and Utah Starzz in the Western Conference.

★ The 1998 Comets team holds the record for highest winning percentage in the history of both the NBA and WNBA. They went 27–3 (.900).

★ Raise the Roof was very much a Houston thing.

★ 1997 attendance: 9,703. 1998 attendance: 12,603. 1999: 11,906. 2000: 12,255.

★ The Comets folded in 2008.

A PERFECT STORM

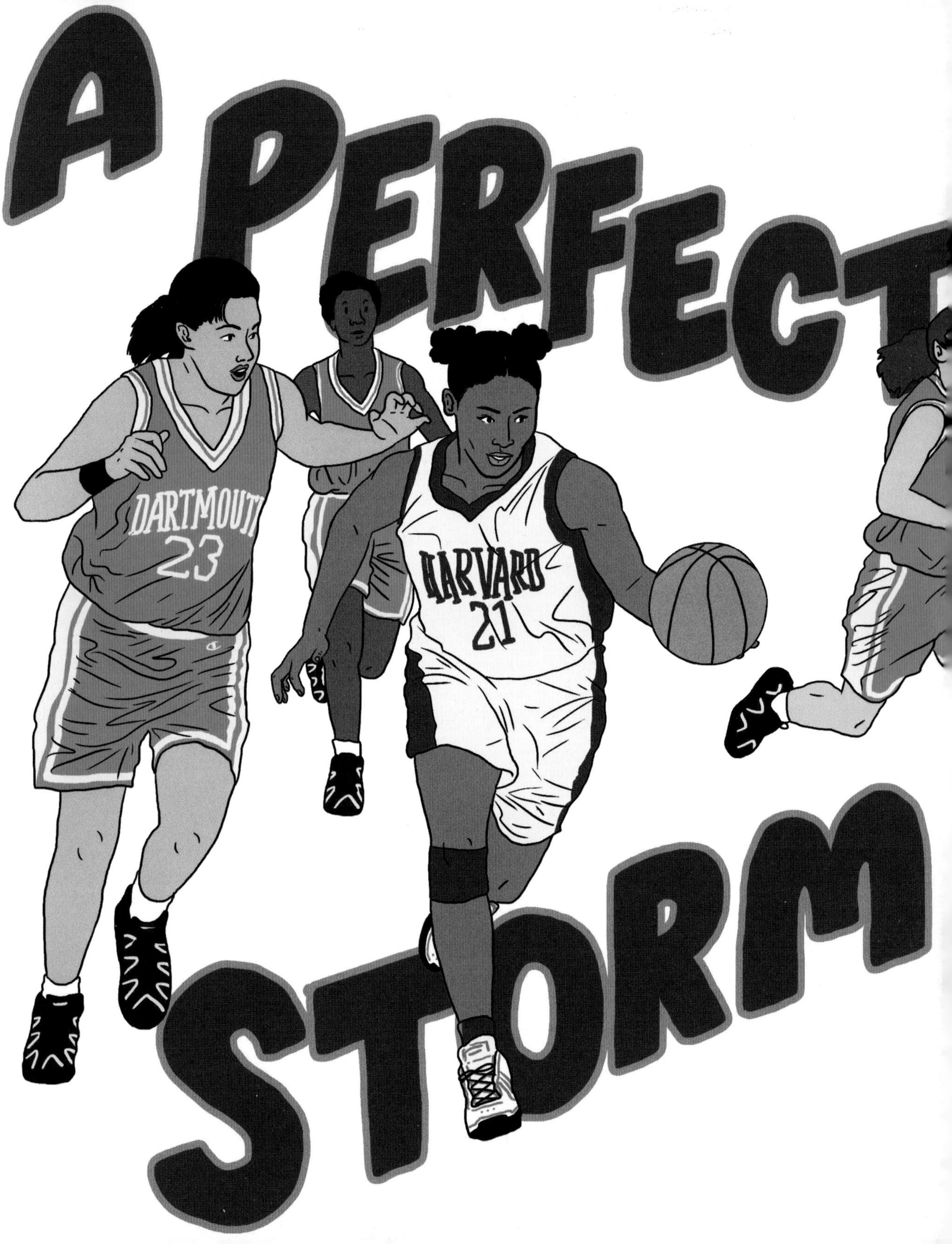

"THE PERFECT STORM"

HOW SIXTEEN SEED HARVARD TOPPLED NUMBER ONE SEED STANFORD IN 1998

As the final seconds ticked away, the scoreboard showed: Harvard 71, Stanford 67. The Crimson players danced in jubilation. The Cardinal's seniors sat stunned on the bench. The game had been played on Stanford's home floor, in front of their own fans. How could this—the biggest upset in sports history—have happened?

"I don't think Harvard was a sixteen seed, and we weren't a one seed," Stanford coach Tara VanDerveer told ABC in 2015, nearly twenty years after her team's historic loss. "They were a very good team: they had a great player, an excellent coach, and I think it was the perfect storm."

When most people heard the news—the first sixteen seed to ever beat a number one seed!—they were missing much of the context. Most still are. See, when Harvard flew across the country to Palo Alto for the first round of the NCAA tournament, their opponent barely resembled the dominant Stanford squad all had come to know. But before we get to Stanford's crippling bad luck, let's focus on Harvard, who probably could have given Stanford a run for its money no matter the circumstances.

Quietly, the Crimson had put together a few fantastic years in the Ivy League. They'd won the Ivy and advanced to the NCAA tournament in 1996 and 1997. And that next year, they were anchored by Allison Feaster, who had been a star since she was a freshman, but as a senior was the leading scorer in the country. Harvard was 22–4 and the squad was

baffled—and angry—as they watched the selection show and saw that they'd been given the worst seed in the tournament. "We all felt disrespected—we thought we were better than a sixteen seed," Harvard coach Kathy Delaney-Smith, who spent forty years as the team's head coach, told ABC. "It was the fuel that fired us, and that was probably where we formed our game plan."

So Harvard was better than a sixteen seed. Meanwhile, in Stanford's final game before the NCAA tournament bracket was announced, senior forward Vanessa Nygaard injured her knee. But the team wouldn't know the severity until an MRI the following day, and so the selection committee—charged with seeding teams—also wasn't sure whether Stanford's star player would be available in the postseason.

Nygaard actually received a call from the doctor while at VanDerveer's house. She was watching the bracket unveiling on ESPN with the rest of the team. On the phone, the doctor confirmed the worst: she'd torn her ACL. But the bracket was already set, and Stanford was already a top seed.

As if that wasn't brutal enough, the next day in practice, two-sport star Kristin Folkl, the team's leading scorer and rebounder, went down with her own knee injury—another torn ACL. "She got clipped in the air and came down awkwardly," VanDerveer told ABC. "She let out a scream, and I thought, 'This is a nightmare.' I remember feeling physically ill. We basically had to stop practice. It was like a morgue in there. No one wanted to keep going."

As Harvard was traveling west, Stanford was reeling. But Harvard was in no mood to throw Stanford a pity party. As Delaney-Smith explained to ABC, she ran into VanDerveer in the parking lot before the game. "She started to talk to me about the injuries. I was like, 'Tara, don't even. If you want sympathy from me, you are not going to get it.' And then one of our assistant coaches went back to our locker room after we started warm-ups and one of the event managers guarding the locker room said, 'Welcome to the world of real basketball.' You know I used that with our team."

Nygaard and Folkl—who averaged a combined thirty-four points per game that year—watched from the sidelines as Harvard stepped onto the floor at Maples Pavilion in front of one of the loudest home crowds in hoops. And despite all this, the injuries and locker room fodder, Harvard still could have been in over its heads. Except that they had Feaster.

The Harvard star finished the game with thirty-five points and thirteen rebounds. "People said she played out of her mind," Delaney-Smith said. "But truth be told, she played like that every single game."

Since then, on the women's side, no sixteen seed has beaten a top seed—nobody has even come close. And if you look at the stars that aligned for Harvard, and the ones that crashed to earth for Stanford, you get a sense of why.

★ Allison Feaster went on to a long career in the WNBA and is now VP of player development for the Boston Celtics.

★ Data from FiveThirtyEight: "Harvard's win was the first and last time a top-three seed lost a first-round game in the NCAA women's tournament. Through 21 years and 252 such games, top-three seeds have won an astounding 99.6 percent of the time (251–1). By comparison, that is the same chance that our statistical model gives Kentucky's men's team to win in its first-round game this year. Overall, the chances of a men's No. 1 seed losing in the first round are about 10 times greater than a women's No. 1 falling to a No. 16 seed."

THEY'RE LIKE THE BEATLES!

THE "THREE MEEKS" AND TENNESSEE'S UNDEFEATED SEASON

To understand how wildly popular the Tennessee Lady Volunteers were in the late nineties, one must understand just one fact: head coach Pat Summitt, known for doing almost anything to promote the game, forbade her players from signing autographs at the 1998 Final Four in Kansas City. (Unless it was an already booked autograph session—she wasn't that cruel!)

Summitt was forced to take this unprecedented step because her squad—the two-time reigning NCAA champs, undefeated, and boasting the world's best player—had spent the entire season navigating excited crowds who would come to their hotels and follow their bus to the arenas. "We started having to travel with a police officer, a security person," said Holly Warlick, who was one of Summitt's assistant coaches. Longtime sports information director Debby Jennings added, "We were like the Beatles."

How had this happened? Well, for one, the aforementioned *world's best player*. That would

be Chamique Holsclaw. For another, Summitt, who in March of that season appeared, with that legendary steely gaze, on the cover of *Sports Illustrated*. And then there was Tennessee's iconic freshman class: Kristen (Ace) Clement, Teresa Geter, Tamika Catchings, and Semeka Randall. These last two players, now paired with Chamique, became affectionately known as the "Three Meeks"—Tamika, Semeka, Chamique.

"It was crazy," said Warlick. "One special thing about those three: Chamique was already here and Semeka and Tamika came to Tennessee not to be The Star, but to help continue building the program. They had a love for the program and a love for Pat and they came in wanting to be better players. They weren't worried about who was scoring the points, they wanted to win, and that's why they got along so well with Pat."

The Lady Vols had lit the basketball world on fire. And although it made sense in retrospect—look again at that freshman quartet!—Tennessee had lost ten games the season before, winning the title only after, earlier in that season, falling out of the top ten for the first time in a decade. That year had been an emotional roller coaster. And so, each time the arena was jamming, and fans were screaming their names, Summitt would nudge the upperclassmen. "Remind the freshmen," she'd say. "Remind them what last year was like."

The anger, the frustration, the kicked trash cans, the crying in the locker room. "Of all our runs to a championship, this one is really the most unexpected," Summitt had said of that 1996–97 title. "It came from a team with tremendous heart and desire."

So that was the foundation, and even in the midst of the frenzy of the following season, the upperclassmen remained grounded. Juniors Kellie Jolly, Niya Butts, and Holdsclaw kept their heads level, even as their eyes popped at the crowds. "They loved it," Warlick said. "It was all new to them. They signed every autograph they had a chance to sign..."—that is, until the Final Four—"they took every picture they could take until we had to go. They didn't say, 'Oh God, I can't get off the bus it's so crowded.' This was a culture that they embraced."

The season started with a whopping thirty-eight-point win over Mississippi at home, in Knoxville. But it was the next game—against number two Louisiana Tech—that made people's heads turn. Why? Because Tennessee was down five in the second half. To shake things up, Summitt put in all four freshmen. The Lady Vols immediately went on a 12–0 run, and it's only a slight exaggeration to say they never again trailed that season.

"Our crowds started getting insane," said one of those freshmen, Semeka Randall. "At home that was normal, but on the road, we started drawing huge numbers, and we were outdrawing the home team. Every time we played, there was a crowd. Every moment was a highlight. The intensity behind it, we were getting everybody's best."

And each team's best was never enough. The closest any team would get, all season, was Alabama, which lost by six points and four points. At the Final Four, in Kansas City, the Lady Vols won the semis *and* finals by eighteen points.

They finished the season 39–0 and were crowned the best team in history...at least until that point. "This team is so good, honestly," Tennessee assistant coach Mickie DeMoss told *Sports Illustrated*. "Now we've created this monster, this standard, and I don't know if we'll be capable of ever repeating this."

★ From Semeka Randall: "That year, my freshman year, we were playing UNC and we were down. Pat was trying to motivate us, Chamique couldn't get it going. Pat calls a timeout and I said, can I say something? Then I say, Chamique, where the hell are you? And the next thing we know Chamique scores fifteen points in a row. Me to snap at Chamique? That doesn't happen in today's game."

★ Semeka explaining how they'd get rowdy in the locker room and chant: "WHO'S IN THE HOUSE TONIGHT, UT, WHO'S IN THE HOUSE, WHO'S IN THE HOUSE, WHO'S IN THE HOUSE, UT UT UT!"

PRESIDENT TAMIKA CATCHINGS
The Unassuming Ambassador

During this legendary undefeated season, surrounded by Tennessee icons like Pat Summitt and Chamique Holdsclaw, Tamika Catchings could sometimes be overlooked. Soft-spoken and shy, she always found her confidence on the court. And of all the big-name players who helped make this iconic season possible, it was Catchings who quietly built a résumé unparalleled in its impact and scope.

On the court, Catchings was a beast. She had offensive finesse, but the heart and wingspan to become one of the game's greatest defenders. By the time she retired in 2016, she was a four-time Olympic gold medalist, a ten-time WNBA all-star, as well as a league MVP and WNBA champion. But those are just numbers. The measure of Catchings is, well, almost impossible to quantify. When she first came into the league—drafted in 2001 by the Indiana Fever— the WNBA hit its most difficult stretch. Teams were folding, the country was in economic crisis, and there was serious concern that the WNBA would not survive. During this crucial era, Catchings served as president of the WNBA Players' Association. Alongside Ruth Riley and Swin Cash, Catchings had to help negotiate a way forward. "I remember in the beginning being so scared," Catchings told the *New York Times*. "For me, it was such a daunting task, like, 'Oh my gosh, I've got to represent all these players.'"

Catchings remained president of the WNBPA until her retirement. She was responsible for helping negotiate two collective bargaining agreements (in 2008 and 2014) and laying the foundation for a strong player's union. Former WNBA president Lisa Borders called Catchings one of the most influential players in league history. "She's maybe the best ever because of all she did on the court," hall of fame coach Lin Dunn told the *Times*. "But my goodness gracious, look at what she did off it."

UCONN VS. NOTRE DAME

THE THIRD-WAVE RIVALRY

When Muffet McGraw walked into the Joyce Center on January 15, 2001, an usher stopped the Notre Dame head coach and said, "Did you hear? It's a sellout."

"And I just got chills," the longtime coach remembered. "It was the first sellout we ever had."

McGraw had been head coach of the Fighting Irish since 1987. She'd grown up outside of Philadelphia and played college hoops at St. Joseph's University, then professionally for the California Dreams of the WBL before the league folded. In her first years in South Bend, only a few dozen people would come watch McGraw's teams. A decade later, 1,000 fans was still a good showing. So, this news—the arena was *sold out!*—was a milestone. It was the first of many.

That afternoon in 2001, Notre Dame was playing number one Connecticut, their Big East rival, the defending national champions, winners of thirty consecutive games. Notre Dame had lost all twelve of their previous meetings with the Huskies. But things felt different that season.

"Those first couple years we weren't able to compete with them," said Ruth Riley, who as a senior was the 2001 Naismith Player of the Year, and who went on to become an Olympian and WNBA Finals MVP. "Might have been talent. But something was different our senior year. Our mindset shifted. We just really felt

like they were coming onto our court, that we had the ability to win this game in a different way than what we had felt before."

The game was on ESPN. It was the network's marquee Martin Luther King Day matchup. Just six years earlier, UConn had been in Notre Dame's shoes. The Huskies had hosted number one Tennessee. Back then, Connecticut was the upstart who'd never been number one, who'd never won a title. A victory that day over the vaunted Lady Vols planted a flag in the ground: UConn was a program to be reckoned with.

Now, Geno Auriemma's program wore the bull's-eye. The Huskies were loaded with talent: Sue Bird, Swin Cash, Asjah Jones, Tamika Williams, Kelly Schumacher, Shea Ralph, Svetlana Abrosimova. Oh, and a talented freshman named...*Diana Taurasi*. But Notre Dame was coming into its own, anchored by five seniors and with a starting lineup—including guards Niele Ivey and Alicia Ratay—all averaging double figures.

"It started at the top," Riley said. "It started with Muffet. Her fiery presence. Her confidence. Her basketball IQ. Everything she brought to the program took on her persona."

Notre Dame was finally ready to take the court against UConn with the pure belief that they could win. And that January day, they did—by a lot. When it was done, they'd blown the Huskies off the court, winning by sixteen points. For the first time in program history, the Fighting Irish were the number one team in the country.

"I'm still kind of shocked," Notre Dame guard Niele Ivey, who is now the program's head coach, said at the time. "I think someone hit me upside my head or something. It's just a great feeling. UConn's a great team and to come out there and have a total team effort is just incredible."

This January game was Notre Dame's assertion: the Irish were ready to trade blows with the mighty UConn. And trade they

**2001–2022
NCAA TOURNAMENT RESULTS
NOTRE DAME VS. UCONN**

2001: NCAA semifinal,
Notre Dame wins 90–75

2011: NCAA semifinal,
Notre Dame wins 72–63

2012: NCAA semifinal,
Notre Dame wins 83–75 in OT

2013: NCAA semifinal,
UConn wins 83–65

2014: NCAA final,
UConn wins 79–58

2015: NCAA final, UConn wins
63–53

2018: NCAA semifinal,
Notre Dame wins 91–89 in OT

2019: NCAA semifinal,
Notre Dame wins 81–76

did—that same season and for decades to come. A couple months after its breakthrough, Notre Dame lost to UConn in the Big East title game, but just a few weeks later the two met again in the NCAA semifinals. Notre Dame won, 90–75, then beat Purdue for the first title in program history.

The book *Bird at the Buzzer* chronicles this legendary year between the two rivals. In it, writer Jeff Goldberg explains, "UConn–Notre Dame III was, in most observers' minds, the de facto national championship game. While the opening act, Purdue–Southwest Missouri State, featured a pair of singular stars—Katie Douglas for Purdue and the NCAA's all-time leading scorer Jackie Stiles of SMS—the completion of the epic UConn–Notre Dame trilogy drew the majority of attention from the gathered national media."

These two teams helped anchor women's basketball for the next twenty seasons. During one amazing, nearly decade-long stretch, Connecticut lost only fifteen games. Eight of them were to Notre Dame.

"I think it helps that Niele [Ivey] was an assistant coach," Riley said of her former teammate, who replaced McGraw as head coach in 2020. "She was a huge part of our success and an integral part of their coaching staff. You had a different level of player, too, when you look at those years with Skylar Diggins in 2011 or so. Not just the talent, but the confidence those players played with. I think every time they stepped onto the floor, they felt they could win, and they had a different swagger about them than maybe my generation. There was an underlying confidence—it had to start somewhere—and it happened to start in those games my senior year in 2001. That was the starting point. But it just accelerated from there."

NOTRE DAME WAS FINALLY READY TO TAKE THE COURT AGAINST UCONN WITH THE PURE BELIEF THAT THEY COULD WIN.

"BIRD AT THE BUZZER"
An Instant Classic

Two months after Notre Dame usurped UConn as the number one team in the country, the two teams met again for the Big East tournament championship. The game was played on Connecticut's home floor. Just two years after it was played, the game became the first in any women's sport to air as an "Instant Classic" on ESPN Classic.

The original game matchup aired on ESPN on March 6, 2001. The game was called by Robin Roberts, with color by Doris Burke. On the court that night were five future Olympians and eight future first-round WNBA draft picks. The game went down to the final seconds. Notre Dame center Ruth Riley hit one of two free throws with 5.1 seconds left to tie the game.

UConn had no timeouts. The Huskies quickly inbounded to guard Sue Bird, who caught the ball already heading downcourt. Bird raced against the clock and darted into the lane, jump-stopped, and made a fadeaway that hit off the front of the rim before dropping through. Here was the game call by Roberts: "My goodness, Sue Bird...the poise to go the length of the floor, create space and make that shot...and the Huskies are the Big East tournament champions. Great effort by Muffet McGraw and the Fighting Irish, but Connecticut would not be denied. Avenging one of their two losses on the year."

On this night, neither team would ever lead by more than eight points. One of UConn's greatest players, Shea Ralph, went down with an ACL tear in the first half. And the final minute saw numerous lead changes and big plays from Bird (a three-pointer with 49.8 seconds left) and Riley. As Roberts trailed off, Burke put the cherry on top, adding, "This is as good a game as you can ask for in women's college basketball."

SHOCK WAVE

BILL LAIMBEER
AND THE BAD GIRLS
LIGHT UP DETROIT, GO
WORST TO FIRST.

For Swin Cash, the memory is still intoxicating: 22,076 passionate fans packed into the Palace at Auburn Hills for the deciding game three of the 2003 WNBA Finals.

"I'm getting chills just thinking about being in that moment," Cash said. "That night, it was something really special. I think the city of Detroit, more than any other WNBA city in that moment in time, they respected us so much, and they showed us their love and respect."

Cash was just a kid when all this went down. The year before, she'd been drafted number two out of UConn, and joined the middling Detroit Shock. The Motor City had been the

first expansion W franchise, but they'd floundered in their first four seasons. Then during Cash's rookie year, the team hit rock bottom, going 9–23. The worst team in the league.

That very bad season could have been even worse. Detroit started the year 0–10 before former NBA bad boy Bill Laimbeer took over as head coach. He lost his first three games (so they were 0–13!), but then finished the season 9–10, and by the end Laimbeer started

to believe that the Shock had the potential to quickly turn around their fortunes. Cash was a young star, and she paired well with Deanna Nolan, who was just a year older and could do a whole lot of everything. Plus, Detroit had the number one pick in the dispersal draft (they took center Ruth Riley) and the number three pick in the regular draft (they took power forward Cheryl Ford).

The entire off-season, Laimbeer stayed in contact with his players. The former Pistons star had a vision. He'd won back-to-back NBA titles with the squad known as the "Bad Boys," and he spent months sharing what he had learned as a player. "Sometimes, with women's basketball, people act like everybody has to get along, or we have to do this emotional deep dive, but with Bill, that was the first time anyone was like, 'Nah, you're going to be treated like pros,'" said Cash. "He shared a lot that first year about the Bad Boys and what it took to win, and that grit and that mindset, but he also had the wherewithal to consistently say, 'It's about the players, you guys have to feel a certain way.'"

No surprise, come that 2003 season, the Shock morphed into a physical, gritty team that didn't back down. The city embraced this new iteration, and the Shock were nicknamed the "Bad Girls." Fans started flocking to games. Radio hosts requested the players. The city was on fire for the Shock. "Were we the most talented team at that point?" Cash said. "No, but we had this mentality of 'We are going to beat you, and beat you, and pound you, and be physical,' and Bill talked about that every day."

Not every player seemed to fit the "Bad Girls" style, but once they arrived in Detroit, something shifted. Take Riley, who had helped Notre Dame to its first-ever NCAA title in 2001, beating Cash's UConn squad along the way. She was physical, sure, but nobody would have dropped a "bad girl" label on Riley. "It's not like Ruth lost her identity, but we started making jokes like, 'Oh, when she put that headband on, she's gonna be out there throwing elbows.' Somehow, she just fit into the mold. We all fit some way into the mold."

Around the league, the Shock weren't really on anyone's radar. Detroit was still very young. The average age of its starting lineup was about twenty-three years old. No pressure existed on them. "It was a ride," Cash said. "And everybody was happy to be in it and doing it together. Nobody was really checking for us."

The Shock started the season 8–1. Around the WNBA, heads whipped to Detroit. And the city started buzzing about their team. "They were talking about us the same way they were talking about the Pistons," Cash said. "There was no in-between, the love was so genuine and real."

The Shock finished the regular season 25–9, the best record in the Eastern

Conference, and had home-court advantage throughout the playoffs. First, they beat the Cleveland Rockers in the opening round, then swept the Connecticut Sun before facing the two-time defending WNBA champs, the Los Angeles Sparks, in the best-of-three WNBA Finals.

The opening game was in Los Angeles, and the Sparks dominated the Shock, winning by twelve points. "I remember coming back to Detroit after getting our heads smacked in LA, and everybody basically being like, 'The Shock have no shot; Lisa Leslie and the crew, they're about to three-peat.'"

In front of nearly 18,000 fans inside the Palace, the Shock eked out a victory in game two, evening up the series, and setting the stage for a legendary game three.

On September 16, 2003, the number of fans who poured into the Palace—that is, 22,076—remains to this day the most people who have ever attended a WNBA game. "If there was any trickling over of the Pistons–Lakers matchups from the NBA side back in the day, then we had all of it full throttle that night," Cash said. "I mean, that was something special. The crowd took us to a whole different place, and never once did I think we would lose."

And they didn't. On that night, Detroit became the only franchise in major sports (men or women) to go from worst to first, and they'd go on to win two more titles under Laimbeer.

"I can still go to Detroit today and even though I've played on a million teams, people will still talk to me about the Detroit Shock and that run and that era," Cash said. "We embodied the whole idea of what the relationship between a franchise and a city is supposed to be."

★ The Sparks were about to become a dynasty. They were anchored by center Lisa Leslie, and had a roster that included DeLisha Milton-Jones, Nikki Teasley, Tamecka Dixon, and Mwadi Mabika.

★ Two WNBA franchises, the Miami Sol and the Portland Fire, folded after the 2002 season. On April 24, the remaining W teams held a draft to distribute the players of both teams. Because Detroit had the league's worst record the year before, it "earned" the top pick.

★ Four years later, in 2007, the Shock would match their attendance record, in a game also played on September 16, and also in the WNBA Finals. The next eight highest-attended WNBA games all took place at the Verizon Center, with the Washington Mystics.

★ Cheryl Ford is the daughter of NBA legend Karl Malone.

★ Deanna Nolan is perpetually underrated.

PASSING THE BATON

JACKIE STILES VS. KELSEY PLUM FOR THE NCAA RECORD BOOKS

⚡

JJackie Stiles is glad that, on the night she broke the NCAA's all-time scoring record—March 1, 2001—she was unaware of all the resources that had gone into the moment.

For example: she didn't know that her school, Southwest Missouri State, had printed more than 10,000 pictures of their legendary guard, emblazoned with that night's date, and congratulating her on breaking the record. Or that Patricia Hoskins, who held the record until that night, had been flown in to witness the moment.

But it's not as if Stiles was oblivious. She knew the heat around her. For more than a year, pretty much everywhere she went in Springfield, Missouri, fans would come up and say hi and let her know how many points she had left before breaking the record. And as she got closer, she couldn't escape it. "I remember I wouldn't let my roommate turn on a TV, or have a paper, or turn the radio on, because it would be all they were discussing," Stiles said. "We went to try to eat at Taco Bell or Burger King—some fast-food restaurant—and we just got mobbed. This was the week before I was projected to break it."

That same week, the school hired a bodyguard to shadow Stiles, who was finding it hard to warm up. Fans were endlessly approaching her, congratulating her, wanting a moment of her time. "And I'll never forget walking into the gym the night I broke the record," Stiles said. "There was tape all lined on the baseline. To get all the media outlets to fit our baseline it had to be *that* organized. It was wild. It seems like a separate life almost."

She needed twenty points that night at home against Creighton, which was doable considering Stiles averaged 30.3 points per game that season. But Creighton was a tough defensive opponent, so it wasn't a given. But the next game was senior night, and Stiles was intent on avoiding stealing the spotlight. She wanted that celebration to stand alone. The five-foot-eight guard wasn't the kind of player who normally counted her points, but on this night, it was inescapable: the sold-out crowd collectively counted her progress with every basket made. When Stiles finally broke the record, she describes the moment as "a big weight at first, and then it was like I was light as a feather when it was over."

The work ethic of Jackie Stiles is legendary. She was a fierce guard with a smooth outside shot, but enough strength to get to the rim, and enough savvy to pull up from mid-range. The stories of her dedication became mythic: she would make 1,000 shots every day. Not take...*make*. Not sometimes...*every day*.

Stiles held the scoring record from that night in 2001 until 2017, when University of Washington guard Kelsey Plum scored fifty-seven points against Utah to pass Stiles on the list. Stiles was planning to attend the following game on the schedule, because that was when Plum was predicted to pass her. Nobody could plan for a fifty-seven-point explosion from the smooth lefty. Stiles watched on TV, and since she knew one of Washington's assistants, she got Plum on the phone after the game to congratulate her.

> **WE WENT TO TRY TO EAT AT TACO BELL OR BURGER KING—SOME FAST-FOOD RESTAURANT—AND WE JUST GOT MOBBED.**
> —JACKIE STILES

STILES AND PLUM WILL ALWAYS BE LINKED. BUT THEIR CONNECTION GOES BEYOND NUMBERS AND SCORING LISTS.

Stiles and Plum will always be linked. But their connection goes beyond numbers and scoring lists.

"I feel like—and I'm not going to take credit—but I feel like I had a hand in at least giving Kelsey that vision that she could one day become the all-time leading scorer," Stiles said.

The story goes like this: Stiles returned to the college game in 2012, accepting an assistant coaching position at Loyola Marymount University. She took the job in July, in the heart of summer recruiting season, and she immediately hit the road. Plum, playing with her Amateur Athletic Union (AAU) team, was one of the first players Stiles observed. "And I will never forget watching her," Stiles remembered. "She's number ten; I was number ten. I saw myself in her. The way she could score—from three, the midrange game, she could take it to the rim, she could go right, she could go left."

"I was like, 'Oh my gosh, I don't care if we don't have a chance of getting her, I must get her on the phone. I had to talk to her. She just mesmerized me.'"

When Stiles, then thirty-four years old, got Plum, then a high school senior, on the phone, the college legend told the star recruit: "Hey, I know you don't know me, but I was the all-time leading scorer and I want to help you break my record."

"That was not a recruiting line," Stiles said. "I genuinely believed that she could do it. I feel like I put that in her head that it was possible because I believe it—I knew she could do it."

★ Top five all-time NCAA scorers: Kelsey Plum (Washington, 3,527), Kelsey Mitchell (Ohio State, 3,402), Jackie Stiles (Missouri State, 3,393), Brittney Griner (Baylor, 3,283), Patricia Hoskins (Mississippi Valley State, 3,122).

★ In 2001, Stiles led Southwest Missouri State to the Final Four, including toppling number one seed Duke—the last mid-major in women's basketball to reach a Final Four.

★ In 2001, Stiles was drafted fourth by the Portland Fire; she was voted that year's Rookie of the Year. But injuries derailed her career.

★ Stiles was a huge fan of Pistol Pete Maravich.

ROLLING IN RUBLES

THE LEGEND OF SPARTAK MOSCOW

The story reads like a movie script. An ex-KGB spy falls in love with a women's basketball player and goes on to bankroll the most successful women's basketball team in the world, lavishing his players with cash and jewelry—treating them like rock stars. Or, rather, like their NBA counterparts have long been treated.

Shabtai von Kalmanovic was the businessman, the former spy, and his team was Spartak Moscow. In 2006, he decided to pay Diana Taurasi and Sue Bird—both UConn and WNBA stars—*a lot* of money to come win his team the European championship. The contracts started at nearly half a million, then, over the years, ballooned past $1 million. The roster was all Russian players, save for the American stars brought over to take the team to the next level.

Over the years, Bird and Taurasi were joined by Aussie legend Lauren Jackson, Tennessee star Tamika Catchings, and others.

And the stories from those years, they've become the stuff of legend. Players living in sprawling villas, with dedicated drivers, and first-class tickets, and chartered flights, and cash bonuses, and surprise trips to St. Petersburg, and gifts of watches and jewelry, and private performances by musicians such as 50 Cent, and caviar and champagne after big wins, and on and on.

The posh life as a women's basketball player on Spartak Moscow ended abruptly in 2009 when Shabtai von Kalmanovic was murdered—shot in his car on the street—outside the Kremlin. To understand exactly how von Kalmanovic viewed his investment in the women's game, we turn to an ESPN article from 2008:

"What is the difference between Barbra Streisand, Madonna and Diana Taurasi?" von Kalmanovic asked between nibbles from a spread of black caviar and blini before a Spartak game. "Madonna, Taurasi—it doesn't make any difference that one is attracting people by singing and the other is attracting people by scoring. Why should Madonna have cars, drivers, security and not our players?"

THE CONTRACTS STARTED AT NEARLY HALF A MILLION, THEN, OVER THE YEARS, BALLOONED PAST $1 MILLION. THE ROSTER WAS ALL RUSSIAN PLAYERS, SAVE FOR THE AMERICAN STARS BROUGHT OVER TO TAKE THE TEAM TO THE NEXT LEVEL.

"WE ARE ALL BG"
The Illegal Detention of Olympian Brittney Griner

Three years after the death of Shabtai von Kalmanovic, a different Russian team—UMMC Ekaterinburg—began paying big money to import American basketball stars. The list of WNBA legends who traveled to play in the eastern Russia city is long: Diana Taurasi, Sue Bird, Yolanda Griffith, DeLisha Milton-Jones. And also, beginning in 2014, former Baylor center and Phoenix Mercury all-star, Brittney Griner. The six-foot-seven Olympian played in Ekaterinburg alongside Taurasi for many years. Even after Taurasi retired from international play in 2017, Griner continued playing for UMMC. Russia was the premier place to play for nearly two decades, paying nearly seven-figure salaries and routinely winning European titles.

But then 2022 changed everything. In February of that year, a month before Russia invaded Ukraine, Griner became ensnared in the world's geopolitics. The Russian authorities detained Griner while she was traveling through Moscow's Sheremetyevo airport enroute to Ekaterinburg, alleging that Griner was carrying in her luggage small amounts of hashish oil. Russia charged the basketball star with drug smuggling, an offense that carried a penalty of up to ten years in prison. In May 2022, the United States designated Griner as "wrongfully detained" and began negotiating for her release.

Back in the US, the WNBA players started a campaign to keep the spotlight on their imprisoned teammate. They launched "We Are BG," explaining that any one of them could have found themselves in Griner's shoes. They launched a website and wrote: "Like many athletes competing in the WNBA, Griner—a two-time Olympic gold medalist— plays abroad during the WNBA off-season for the love of the sport, but also in exchange for potentially bigger contracts, which are not available to women's basketball players in the US. Pay inequity has led to Brittney Griner's wrongful detention in Russia, where she is being used as a political pawn."

"THE KISS"

BEHIND THE SCENES ON THE ICONIC MOMENT

Diana Taurasi and Seimone Augustus first started playing against each other as kids, on the AAU circuit. Seimone was a prodigy, playing up two age levels; Taurasi was already a legend in the making, a generational talent from the jump. Even back then, Taurasi was known for her smoothness, as well as what Augustus calls her "trickery." At the free throw line, for example, Taurasi would be the player giving the opponent a little pinch—literally. She'd reach over and pinch Augustus. Mind games were always in Taurasi's repertoire.

Fast-forward to 2013. Both players are in their primes. Augustus and Taurasi are a year removed from starring together on Team USA, winning a gold medal at the 2012 London Olympics. It's late September, the heart of the WNBA playoffs, and two rival teams are battling for the Western Conference title: the Minnesota Lynx (and Augustus) versus the Phoenix Mercury (and Taurasi). "The intensity of a playoff game is through the roof," Augustus explained.

Minnesota head coach Cheryl Reeve has given Augustus the assignment to defend Taurasi, and to pick her up three-quarter court. Everywhere Taurasi went, there was Augustus. The Lynx were focused on denying the ball, limiting the star's touches, and Augustus could see Taurasi's mounting frustration. "As a competitor who's played against her so many times, you know when she's getting to a certain point of frustration," Augustus said. "She'll start throwing a few elbows here and there, just connecting a little. And from time to time, I would

connect back. That's the nature of competition. You throw a 'bow; I throw a 'bow."

The famous play actually happened away from the ball. Augustus was guarding Taurasi around the top of the key, when the Mercury star dished it off to a teammate with her left hand, simultaneously swiping away at Augustus. Taurasi then purposefully walked into Augustus, who held her ground. Taurasi stepped forward again, the pair now inches apart. "Then I hear people yelling, 'Stand your ground!' and the fans were into it, yelling from the stands. And I'm just standing there and we're all huffing and puffing."

And the next moment is pure Taurasi magic. Sure, Augustus and Taurasi are rivals, and fiercely competitive with each other, but there's no animosity. Neither of them actually wants to fight. But there they are, each standing tall, face-to-face, inches from each other. How to back down without...backing down?

"Dee leans in and she says, 'Take that with you, baby' and gives me a kiss, then she just walked off and we both laughed," Augustus said. "Because in typical Dee fashion she was able to de-escalate a situation that could have gotten out of hand, depending on what the next move was."

The referee hit Augustus and Taurasi with a double technical foul, which Taurasi clearly thought was ridiculous. But within seconds the two rivals (and friends) were smiling and laughing.

So what did Taurasi mean when she told Augustus to *take that with you, baby*? "We were making the game difficult for her, and in order for her to reverse that, she wanted to say something to throw the opponent off, and I think that's what it was," Augustus said. "I didn't want to fight; Dee didn't want to fight. But in the arena, you have to show some strength, some confidence. I think it was her trying to capture me and flip me—get in *my* head."

"The Kiss," as it became known, caught the attention of the media—for all kinds of reasons. The moment was written up in most publications, from coast to coast. After the game, in the press conference, Taurasi was asked about the moment, and she deadpanned, "We were just trying to make sweet love." A few minutes later, Augustus countered by telling reporters, "The tango dance that we had; I always say she just wanted some of my deliciousness."

Whether purposely or not, both players were hinting at the larger context of the

BUT THERE THEY ARE, EACH STANDING TALL, FACE-TO-FACE, INCHES FROM EACH OTHER. HOW TO BACK DOWN WITHOUT... BACKING DOWN?

situation. Here they were, the biggest stars in the WNBA, a league that had long shied away from acknowledging—let alone celebrating—the fact that a significant percentage of its players are gay. It's almost as if Augustus and Taurasi were offering a wink and a nod to this subtext, while keeping the moment playful and elevated. Taurasi was almost *daring* someone to ask a follow-up question.

Stripped of all that age-old baggage, The Kiss was, at its core, a beautiful moment: two ultra-competitors who, for a long second, allowed the passion of the game to swell between them, eclipsing even their friendship. Then, with a peck on the cheek, the love and respect came flooding back.

"CHANGE STARTS WITH US"

THE MINNESOTA LYNX TAKE A STAND

The Minnesota Lynx were in Connecticut, preparing to play the Sun, when their home city was rocked by the police killing of two Black men within twenty-four hours, one of whom was shot in Minneapolis. The players were a thousand miles from home, and the energy was dark—the day was dark. The team met for video in their hotel, and Lynx head coach Cheryl Reeve had tears in her eyes. She asked her players how they were feeling; were they even able to focus on basketball right then?

Then she added, "If y'all want to do something, stand up and say something, I'll support you." The coach's words jump-started a team-wide conversation. And this wasn't just any team; the Lynx were the defending WNBA champs and winners of three titles in the previous five years. This team was a dynasty, featuring legends Seimone Augustus, Sylvia Fowles, Maya Moore, Lindsay Whalen, and Rebekkah Brunson. Inside that hotel room in Connecticut, the entire team decided that when they returned to Minnesota, at their next home game, they would make a bold statement—they would wear warm-up shirts with a message.

On the front, the shirts said, "Change Starts with Us," then underneath, "Justice and Accountability." The back featured the names of Philando Castile and Alton Sterling, the two men killed by police, as well as recognizing the five police officers killed in Dallas, known as the Dallas 5. (The 2016 shooting of Dallas police officers also injured nine others.)

Until this moment, no WNBA team had publicly protested racial injustice. And keep in mind, this was months before San Francisco 49ers quarterback Colin Kaepernick first took a knee during the national anthem before NFL games. The simple existence of the WNBA had always been a political statement: women, and predominantly Black women, carving out space for themselves within the (often) sexist world of sports. But what the Lynx had decided to do in July 2016 was an overt statement that everyone on the team, regardless of race, supported. "That was the first display of activism from the WNBA, period," said Augustus. "I can't remember a time before then that a player stood up for any different cause."

Of course, WNBA players had always wanted to address issues of inequity. But they were often told, in the early existence of the league, that the foundation wasn't strong enough to survive political demonstration. "For so long, we didn't say anything, and we kept our mouths closed in fear," Augustus said. "You always heard, 'The league is going to fold; we ain't making no money,' so the fear that came along with *that* was don't say too much, because that might do something to cause the whole league to go under."

On July 9, 2016, the four stars of the Lynx—Whalen, Augustus, Moore, and Brunson—walked into the press conference in those black t-shirts. They didn't alert the league office. They didn't ask for permission. "Because to be honest," Augustus said, "when things need to get done, they just need to get done. When you need to spark a fire, you spark it. You don't even think about it. And that's what happened."

Before the game, the players were told that if they continued with their protest, the off-duty Minneapolis police officers who provided security would likely walk off in protest. This news didn't deter the team. "We as a nation can decide to stand up for what is right, no matter your race, background, or social status," Moore told reporters gathered that night. "It is time that we take a deep look at our ability to be compassionate and empathetic to those suffering from the problems that are deep within our society. Again, this is a human issue, and we need to speak out for change together."

Around the league, other teams took notice of what the Lynx had done. Players looked at Minnesota and asked themselves, "What can we do to help make change?" A few other teams, including New York, Phoenix, and Indiana, wore black shirts during warm-ups. At first, the protests didn't sit well with the WNBA league office, and then-commissioner

Lisa Borders announced that each team would be fined $5,000 and each player $500. On the books was a rule that WNBA uniforms could not be altered, but the news of top-down fines only galvanized the players. Soon, Borders withdrew the fines and explained the decision to the *New York Times*. "While we expect players to comply with league rules and uniform guidelines, we also understand their desire to use their platform to address important societal issues," Borders said. "Given that the league will now be suspending play until August 26 for the Olympics, we plan to use this time to work with our players and their union on ways for the players to make their views known to their fans and the public."

This was the moment, conceived of in a Connecticut hotel room, that changed the WNBA and its players. Not only was their league sturdy enough to sustain protest, but also, possibly, it could become stronger for it. And four years later, as the world faced a pandemic and another racial reckoning, WNBA players already knew exactly what they must do.

★ The Lynx were WNBA champs in 2011, 2013, 2015, and 2017.

THE SIMPLE EXISTENCE OF THE WNBA HAD ALWAYS BEEN A POLITICAL STATEMENT: WOMEN, AND PREDOMINANTLY BLACK WOMEN, CARVING OUT SPACE FOR THEMSELVES WITHIN THE (OFTEN) SEXIST WORLD OF SPORTS.

THE
WEEKENDER
NOTRE
Dame
CHERISH
TREASURE
PAMPER
SOUTH BEND,
INDIANA
NOTRE DAME
24
2018
NCAA
SEMIFINAL
clock is at
3... 2... 1...
3-POINTER
AT THE
"BUZZER"
#5
Arike
Ogunbowale
- FINAL FOUR -

THE WEEKENDER

ARIKE OGUNBOWALE WITH A FINAL FOUR FOR THE AGES

Arike Ogunbowale and her teammates were busing back to South Bend, Indiana—the NCAA championship trophy in the front seat— as the Notre Dame junior spoke on the phone to *TIME* about the all-time weekend she'd just pulled off.

First, the star guard hit a long jumper in the final seconds of the 2018 NCAA semifinal, sending the Fighting Irish past unbeaten UConn; then, two nights later, she hit a turn-around three-pointer at the buzzer to win the title over Mississippi State. The question Arike was asked was: how many? As in, how many times had she watched her game-winning shot?

"I can't even count how many," Ogunbowale told the magazine. "A lot. I keep getting tagged in the video, so I keep watching it. I'm just like, this is insane how this happened."

In the NCAA championship game, Notre Dame had the ball along their own sideline with three seconds remaining, the score tied at 58. Ogunbowale wasn't even the first option. Jessica Shepard was dominating in the post, but Mississippi State doubled her down low. Ogunbowale broke toward the ball as a secondary option, and the rest is (recent) history. "When the shot went in, I couldn't believe it actually," she told *TIME*. "It was just, 'wow,' then I started running to my teammates. After, I heard the whistle. I was like, 'Wait, did I get it off in time?' But I clearly got it off in time. But I was just like, something had to have gone wrong. There's just no way."

It would be impossible to overstate how epic these two shots were—on multiple levels. The college game often gets the rap of lacking parity, of being too predictable. *Just another UConn blowout* was a common refrain. The previous six NCAA titles games had all been decided by ten points or more. So, watching back-to-back Final Four games that went down to the last fraction of a second was a welcome relief. And also, the quality of those finishing possessions was the stuff of legend. The games could have been close, but still ended on a miss. But no, they ended on made shots—of incredibly difficult degree.

To top it off: both jumpers came from the hand of one player! Hollywood couldn't write a better script.

Notre Dame head coach Muffet McGraw was crouched in front of the team bench just inches from where Ogunbowale took the fadeaway three. "The shot went up right in front of us," McGraw told the *Sporting News*. "It was right in front of our bench, so we saw the whole thing, the trajectory. You never know with those kinds of shots. I didn't immediately think, 'That's in.' I just watched it go, and just being in that moment of waiting to see what was going to happen."

What some people don't remember is that, the year before, Ogunbowale had the ball in the final seconds against Stanford, with a trip to the Final Four on the line. Her shot was blocked at the buzzer. Of course, McGraw remembered what had happened just one season prior. "She's the kind of person who can handle moments like that," the legendary coach said.

There was something magical about that 2018 weekend. It belongs to Ogunbowale, yes, but also to the kid in all of us. The one who spent hours outside, counting down (*"and the clock is at 3, it's at 2…1"*) and launching our own game-winning three-pointers. Ogunbowale lived this dream.

"I was always having fun, when working out, doing a lot of crazy different shots," she told *TIME*. "Pounding down, at last second. But to actually do it on a stage like this is unheard of. It's crazy. Really, anything is possible. Keep shooting those crazy, off-balance shots. Because you never know when they're going to come in handy."

BREAKAWAY

MAYA MOORE, ONE OF THE GREATEST OF ALL TIME, CHANGES COURSE

In 2013, Maya Moore visited the White House. It was her fifth visit. Moore had just won her second WNBA title with the Minnesota Lynx—she would go on to win again in 2015 and 2017—and President Barack Obama noted how many times Moore had been invited to his home. Since he had been in office, five times: twice with the University of Connecticut, once with Team USA, and twice with the Lynx.

"Basically, there's like a Maya Moore wing in the White House," Obama joked that day. "When she comes, we've got all her stuff here. She's got a toothbrush."

In 2017, on the heels of her fourth title with Minnesota and second gold medal with Team USA, *Sports Illustrated* named Moore its inaugural "Performer of the Year" and called her "the greatest winner in the history of women's basketball." But it was the next line of that article that hinted at Moore's future: "After adding yet another title to her ridiculously

glorious résumé and vowing to ramp up her game, Maya Moore is also using her status as a sports celebrity to fight for social justice."

A year and a half later, at just twenty-nine years old, Moore announced she would not be playing the upcoming WNBA season. She wrote in the *Players' Tribune*, "There are different ways to measure success. The success that I've been a part of in basketball truly blows my mind every time I think about it. But the main way I measure success in life is something I don't often get to emphasize explicitly through pro ball. I measure success by asking, 'Am I living out my purpose?'"

Moore gave no clear explanation for her departure. The announcement stunned WNBA fans and even those close to Moore, including her coach at UConn. "We were all taken aback," Geno Auriemma told the *New York Times*. "I thought, 'Hey, what is wrong? Is there something Maya is trying to be private about? Is it personal?' I am still just really, really surprised."

What Moore did not explicitly say in that *Players' Tribune* article, but would become clear in just a few months, was that she had left the game to dedicate herself to freeing a man she believed had been wrongfully imprisoned. His name was Jonathan Irons. He'd been convicted at the age of sixteen for burglary and assault, and he'd served twenty-two years of a fifty-year sentence. Moore's family had been connected to Irons through a prison ministry when Moore was still in high school. Moore first visited him before she left for UConn.

Moore felt that focusing on this single case could expose broader corruption in the judicial system. She skipped the following season, 2020, as well. She was a fixture inside Missouri's courtrooms, where Irons was seeking to overturn his 1998 conviction. And on March 9, 2020, a Missouri judge granted Irons's petition, vacating his conviction. Four months later, he was released from prison. Moore was there to greet him. For a moment, she fell to her knees in disbelief.

"There were times that I was ready to give up and just push everybody away," Irons told *Glamour* in 2021. "But their love for me just kept me going—so much that I studied law while I was in prison. I learned how to read it and write it, I helped other prisoners, I helped advocate for rights within the prison. And I was able to write my habeas petition, the first draft of which led to my freedom."

The pair were married very soon after Irons was freed and announced their nuptials on *Good Morning America*. A few months later, Moore responded to a question about her basketball future. "I'm not thinking about that at all right now," she told the Associated Press. "This whole thing has been so unexpected. When Jonathan got home it was like OK, now the rest can start in a way. That's what we've been doing. The story is unfolding still. This is where we're at right now, living in the present."

While Moore was fighting for Irons's release, she appeared on the PBS show *Amanpour & Company*, and was asked about athlete activism. "Athletes are human beings first and foremost," she said. "We are citizens. We are more than what we do on the screen. When we take time to stand up for people and to shine a light in a dark place, not everybody is going to like it when it costs your comfort or maybe something that you just want to check out and enjoy—I get that—entertainment is a place you want to relax and not have to think about the cares of the world, but we are in the world and the world is broken."

★ The EGOT—Emmy, Grammy, Oscar, Tony—of the sports world is winning an NCAA, WNBA, Olympic, and EuroLeague title. Moore has won all four.

★ Moore was included in *TIME*'s 100 *Most Influential People of 2020*.

★ Quote from Moore's acceptance speech at the 2021 ESPYs, where she won the Arthur Ashe Courage Award: "Power is not meant to be gripped with a clenched fist or to be hoarded. Power is meant to be handled generously so we can thoughtfully empower one another to thrive in our communities, for love's sake."

★ The documentary *Breakaway*, telling Moore and Irons's story, premiered on ESPN in July 2021.

THE
144

SAY HER NAME AND
THE BUBBLE SEASON OF 2020

"This is the hardest championship anyone will ever win. The bubble, the state of the world..."

These were the words of WNBA star Chiney Ogwumike in the ESPN documentary *144*, about the 2020 WNBA season, played in the middle of the pandemic and just months after the killing of George Floyd by Minneapolis police set off worldwide protests against racial injustice.

The 2020 W season started more than two months later than originally scheduled. After numerous negotiations between W players and the league office, a plan was established: a twenty-two-game season at the IMG Academy in Florida. Teams would play twenty-two games in forty-nine days. Each franchise could have twelve players and eight staff members inside the bubble. Rigorous COVID-19 testing would be done and protocols would be followed. And, most important, the players would play for something bigger: Breonna Taylor, whose killing by the Louisville, Kentucky, police had sparked outrage. "If we were going to play, we wanted to take our stand on what we believe in," said that year's MVP, A'ja Wilson of the Las Vegas Stars, in *144*.

The season opened on July 25, 2020, with a triple-header. Emblazoned on the IMG court was "Black Lives Matter," and players wore shirts with "Say Her Name"—referencing

Taylor—printed on them. The days inside the "wubble" (a portmanteau of women and bubble) were long and hard. Many players were without their partners, or children, and struggles with anxiety and depression were ubiquitous. The air was heavy.

"The bubble was an eye-opener for me," Las Vegas star Dearica Hamby told ESPN. "Before the bubble I never thought of myself as someone who struggled with mental health. I also never had enough time to sit with myself and only myself, so maybe I wasn't aware."

But the women knew how important the moment was. And so they persevered. Basketball was the platform, but it wasn't the message. "Had we not had a season, sadly, our voices just wouldn't have been heard...the only way to make it happen is to play basketball," WNBA legend Sue Bird said at the time.

And their voice *was* heard. Because they stuck together and made decisions as a unit: a 144. "The state of the world has, for me, shifted in a way that I view the 144 women in this league less as opponents and more as comrades," Nneka Ogwumike, president of the WNBA players' association, told the *Athletic*. "I think that a lot of us have kind of geared or shifted into that frame of thinking and

THE PLAYERS STAYED IN LOCKSTEP WITH ONE ANOTHER AND NEVER LOST SIGHT OF THE LARGER VISION.

understanding that we're all, in a way, one in the same. We're all in this together, we all want to make this work and we all have to trust each other."

The W made headlines throughout the truncated season. The players stayed in lockstep with one another and never lost sight of the larger vision: to support the fight for racial justice and to grow the WNBA so they could leave it a better place for the next generation. "Every game that we played this season was a chance to be in front of an audience and we wanted to educate them about something that we were fighting for," the Seattle Storm's Alysha Clark told Yahoo.

After it was all over, and the Storm had defeated the Aces for the 2020 W title, the trajectory of the league had shifted upward. WNBA commissioner Cathy Engelbart dropped the eye-opening numbers: a 30 percent increase in cross-platform social engagement and a 68 percent increase in viewership across network.

The 144 were soaring.

REAL CHANGE
The Warnock Tees

In early July 2020, the WNBA announced that its upcoming season would be dedicated to Black Lives Matter and focused on advocating for justice for women and girls. In response to this news, Atlanta Dream co-owner Kelly Loeffler wrote a letter to W commissioner Cathy Engelbart. But Loeffler was more than just an owner. She was a senator, appointed by Georgia governor Brian Kemp in November 2019 and up for election in the fall of 2020.

In Loeffler's letter to the WNBA commissioner she expressed her disdain for Black Lives Matter and the W's decision to align with the group. "The truth is, we need less—not more politics in sports," Loeffler wrote. "In a time when polarizing politics is as divisive as ever, sports has the power to be a unifying antidote. And now more than ever, we should be united in our goal to remove politics from sports."

After many public responses, WNBA players realized that Loeffler was capitalizing on this battle with the W. It was a political game. "It was like, 'oh s–t,'" Seattle Storm point guard Sue Bird told *TIME*. "The more we fight her—people were asking, 'Should she be an owner?'—the more we were basically calling for her head, the more it was just playing into her hands."

The players pivoted. Instead of focusing on Loeffler, why not support the opponent running against her? They consulted with politician and voting rights activist Stacey Abrams and vetted a candidate, Raphael Warnock. "After that, players were like, 'O.K., this guy's legit,'" Elizabeth Williams, player for the Dream, told *TIME*. "He was so confident."

Bird suggested the players wear "Vote Warnock" shirts before their games inside the bubble. They would be black with white letters. The players had been garnering increasing attention for their fashion. Specifically, the walk from team bus to locker room. On August 4, dozens of W players rocked the t-shirts, sparking dozens more headlines, and a flood of donations (more than $200K) to Warnock's campaign. These women had provided a huge political push, and come November, Warnock ousted Loeffler, becoming Georgia's first Black US senator.

"We were definitely the loudest voice," said Atlanta shooting guard Tiffany Hayes. "We were the sternest voice. And we backed what we said. I don't see any other hand that was bigger."

THE HOODIE

That Turned a Million Heads

ORIGIN OF THE
WNBA'S BEST-SELLING
PIECE OF GEAR

The seeds of the phenomenon were planted during a routine exchange in 2019. Kobe Bryant had visited the WNBA league offices in New York City, and as he was leaving, Eb Jones handed the legend three bags of W gear, including a statement orange hoodie with the WNBA silhouette.

At the time, Jones oversaw the league's content and influencer strategy. Delivering the gear to Kobe was a Hail Mary—no way would Kobe wear the orange hoodie, Jones assumed. Jones had hand-selected the sweatshirt to become the league's signature piece, although she wavered on the choice because the W plays in the summer. Nobody would want a hoodie during the summer, she reasoned. But then again, the piece was bold and simple. She kept coming back to it. "The hoodie was a simple design that looks good on everybody and was gender-neutral," Jones told *Sports Illustrated*.

In partnership with ESPN, Jones and the W sent out hundreds of orange hoodies to players in the W and the NBA, as well as influencers (and women's sports advocates) like Gabrielle Union and Robin Roberts. The first big moment for the hoodie came in August 2019 when Las Vegas Aces star, and future WNBA MVP, A'ja Wilson wore the orange sweatshirt on the sidelines while injured. "And that's what first started the frenzy," Jones told *SI*.

But at that point, the hoodie was still just a piece of gear. A popular piece of gear, yes, but nothing more. Then three things happened,

one uplifting, the next two tragic. At the end of December, in 2019, Kobe sat courtside at the Staples Center with his daughter Gianna. He wore a Philadelphia Eagles beanie and...the

orange hoodie. "It was just a fan thing before he wore it," Jones said. "But when Kobe wore it, it became a fashion statement."

When Kobe and Gianna died, along with seven others, in a helicopter crash less than a month later, that photo of Kobe in the WNBA hoodie was used in thousands of media reports. It was one of the last photos ever taken of him with his daughter. And suddenly the hoodie came to mean so much more: it became a symbol of supporting women, investing in women, and honoring the connection that Kobe had with his daughter, as well as with the women's game.

Six weeks after the devastating helicopter crash, the world was hit with the COVID pandemic. The NBA season was paused. As summer approached, both the NBA and the WNBA planned to play their seasons in single locations that eventually came to be known as "the bubble" and "the wubble"—that is, the women's

It was more than a hoodie. J, it was a movement.

I need one.

bubble. Jones, with the help of ESPN, sent out 150 hoodies to men's players, as well as influencers, in advance of the WNBA season. On the opening day of the season, the #orangehoodie was everywhere: on LeBron James, Chris Paul, Devin Booker, Jayson Tatum, Damian Lillard, rapper Lil Wayne, and tennis star Naomi Osaka.

Over the next year, the hoodie became the best-selling item on the entire Fanatics website, as well as the best-selling WNBA item in history. "It's a lie that the W doesn't sell," Jones told Yahoo! Sports. "The W does sell."

KOBE AND GIANNA

A REVERBERATING LOSS

The scene is both universal and iconic: a father sitting courtside, coaching his young daughter in the game they both love. This interaction has played out a million times over the years, between dads and daughters across the world. But what made this so singular was the dad: eighteen-time NBA all-star, and Los Angeles Lakers legend, Kobe Bryant; and the daughter, Gianna Bryant, with her sights set on someday playing for Geno Auriemma at the University of Connecticut, then the WNBA afterward.

Kobe and Gianna were a duo: he, one of the coaches for her AAU team at the Mamba Sports Academy that he helped launch in 2018; she, the heir apparent to his legacy. He was on the sidelines for her games, and they were on the sidelines together to watch the best in the world—the WNBA. "There's no better way to learn than to watch the pros do it," Kobe told the *New York Times* after bringing Gianna and her Mamba AAU teammates to watch the Los

Angeles Sparks play the Las Vegas Aces. "The WNBA is a beautiful game to watch."

One of the last images taken of them together was courtside at an NBA game, Kobe wearing the bright orange WNBA hoodie. He was pointing out game strategy to his daughter, his arm draped over her shoulder. A month later, the two of them, along with seven others, would die in a helicopter crash while traveling to a game at the Mamba Academy.

On that day, so much was lost. And one piece of the grief was for a future that would now never exist: Gianna Bryant, growing with the game, excelling at different levels. Alongside her, of course, would have been Kobe, shining a spotlight on the women's game. In fact, they were already doing it. In 2019, Kobe stopped by the W headquarters in New York to meet with the league office and discuss the WNBA's future. In the off-season, up-and-coming high school and college stars like Hailey Van Lith would work out at Mamba Academy. And when the Oregon Ducks came to Los Angeles to play Southern California, Kobe and Gigi were sitting courtside to see Oregon's Sabrina Ionescu, the best college player in the country. From that day forward, Ionescu considered Kobe a mentor. "We got to become really, really close friends," Ionescu said on the *Sports Uncovered* podcast. "We talked a few times a week. We talked really about everything whether it was basketball, his family, my basketball. Really the conversation took us wherever we really wanted."

After their deaths, former Cal player Talia Caldwell wrote an opinion piece for the *New York Times*. Here are her final two paragraphs of that piece:

What Kobe did, consciously or not, was give male sports fans a curiosity about why an all-time N.B.A. great found so much joy and pleasure in women's basketball. He spent time with W.N.B.A. players, who were his peers. He casually mentioned their names in interviews, tweets and Instagram posts, prompting people to learn about the world-class athletes that they were late to discover.

Kobe Bryant, the scorer, the ultimate alpha, was ridiculed his entire career for not passing the ball enough. I hope he's remembered for passing the ball to women.

THE WHITE MAMBA
Taurasi and Kobe

Kobe was, of course, known as the Black Mamba. He bestowed a similar nickname on WNBA legend Diana Taurasi. She was early in her career when Bryant said of the Phoenix Mercury star, "She's a Mamba. The white one," and from then on Taurasi took on the nickname "The White Mamba."

In his book, *The Mamba Mentality: How I Play*, Bryant outlined his philosophy. The cornerstones were resilience, fearlessness, obsessiveness, relentlessness, and passion. It's no surprise that Kobe saw himself in Taurasi, who embodies all those traits. Taurasi has never joined social media, because (among other reasons) she believes it a distraction to getting better, to being present. She went vegan later in her career to preserve her joints and elevate her physical fitness—all with the goal of extending her career.

And the White Mamba was as deadly on the court as her male counterpart. The two blazed trails in their respective leagues—and through opponents. And as fate would have it, Taurasi stood poised to break the W's all-time scoring record while playing on the road in her hometown of Los Angeles in June 2017. Tina Thompson held the record until the White Mamba made a driving layup for her 7,489th career point. Taurasi was presented the game ball and given a standing ovation. The crowd included Kobe, with a daughter on each side.

Taurasi had grown up a diehard Lakers fan. She studied Kobe's game. "On the nights the Lakers played, I wouldn't miss a second of the game," Taurasi said at Kobe's memorial service in 2020. "Every timeout, every commercial, I'd run to the front yard to imitate my favorite Laker, Kobe. He made it okay to play with an edge that bordered on crazy."

HOMECOMING

CANDACE PARKER
RETURNS TO CHICAGO AND
DELIVERS A TITLE

Candace Parker tells a story about her freshman year at the University of Tennessee. She has had knee surgery and can't play. The transition to college is tough. Back home in Chicago, her parents are getting a divorce. Nothing is easy. Amid this, Tennessee head coach Pat Summitt invites Parker to come by her office every Wednesday at lunch.

"By the third session, it was like therapy for me," Parker told *Chicago* magazine in 2021. "We talked about life and how we dealt with stuff. She was the one who really helped me through everything. And she was ahead of her time in terms of advice. She'd say, 'I'm going to tell you what you need to hear, not necessarily what you want to hear.'"

> **PLAYING OUT THE REST OF HER CAREER IN LA? THAT SEEMED THE EASIEST CHOICE. THEY'D WON A WNBA TITLE IN 2016 AND WERE ALWAYS IN THE HUNT FOR ANOTHER. BUT PARKER ISN'T ABOUT EASY.**

Get comfortable with being uncomfortable, Parker explained, is a phrase she tries to live by.

Staying in Los Angeles, where Parker played the first thirteen seasons of her WNBA career, would have been the comfortable choice. The franchise had drafted her number one in 2008, just after Parker had led the Lady Vols to back-to-back titles (and the seventh and eighth in program history). Playing out the rest of her career in LA? That seemed the easiest choice. They'd won a WNBA title in 2016 and were always in the hunt for another. But Parker isn't about easy.

Historically, player movement in the WNBA has been limited. Some of that was baked into the actual language of the league agreements—for example, a team could "core" a player, which meant their free agency status was revoked—and some was because of the relatively low contracts. Unlike in the NBA, one team couldn't woo another team's star with some outlandish offer. Everything was very cookie cutter.

But in the summer of 2021, things shifted, in part because of the new collective bargaining agreement (CBA) the league and players had signed, and in part because of *who* was hitting the free agency market that summer. That is, Candace Parker.

As free agency opened, there were whispers about big names changing teams, but most believed that's all it would be, whispers. But the Chicago Sky had other plans. The team and coach James Wade believed they needed a player like Parker to take their franchise to the next level. So they pursued her—hard. Wade flew to Atlanta and pitched Parker on the Sky, and when the news broke in February that Parker was coming home, the WNBA world was on fire. "Really nobody has ever signed a free agent like this," Wade told the *Chicago Tribune* that day. "For us to be the team that has the biggest free-agency signing in league history is special."

The storytelling was clear, with Wade saying this is "an incredible story of a homecoming between a team striving to become a championship organization and one of the best players in basketball." After Parker signed, she sent a text message to teammates Allie Quigley and Courtney Vandersloot, writing, "We're right there. We have it right there, like we have it right there and we can realize our dreams."

The signing would draw comparisons to LeBron James's 2014 decision to return to Cleveland. Parker was a two-time MVP. But could she deliver the first WNBA title to her hometown?

As the 2021 season began, things didn't look so good. Parker missed nine games with an ankle injury. The team had both a seven-game win streak and seven-game losing streak. "I feel like we were frustrated with ourselves, with each other, and it was because we didn't know who we were," Quigley said during a postgame press conference.

The Sky finished the regular season 16–16. But as the postseason began, everything that had been up in the air seemed to land exactly in place. Parker was on the court. The team was gelling. And in the first round of the playoffs, they dominated the top-seeded Connecticut Sun. The world was on notice.

When Chicago defeated the Phoenix Mercury in the WNBA Finals, Parker stood in front of a sold-out arena. Through tears, she tried to explain the moment to ESPN's Holly Rowe: "It's amazing, look at this, it's amazing. My high school coach is here, I know Pat [Summitt] is watching. I got the whole city here; *we* got the whole city here. And it's just amazing how Chicago supports. We're champions for life now."

Parker came home on a mission. And she delivered.

★ "I was about to take my daughter to a basketball game when I heard about Kobe. It was one of those moments that rock the entire world, when you're always going to remember what you were doing. He really let us see who he was during his last couple of years. He let us see the joy and the laughter instead of always being serious. He was an entire human, not just a basketball player, and I kind of fell in love with the part of him that was a father who brought his daughter around to different tournaments. And so I think that's what's been so hard to move past. All of us, especially athletes, can see ourselves in him. I still wake up and can't believe it. It doesn't seem real."—Candace Parker in *Chicago* magazine.

★ "A couple of years ago, I was voted the most overrated player in the WNBA. It was a poll by the *Athletic*. Players voted. I laughed because it's almost comical. But honestly, it just gives me more motivation on a random Tuesday to wake up and work out. That's what I'm taking from it."—Candace Parker in *Chicago* magazine.

THE SHOT(S)

The Ten Most Iconic Shots in Basketball History

(NOT ALREADY REFERENCED WITHIN)

PLAYER: Teresa Weatherspoon

TIME LEFT ON CLOCK: At the buzzer

WHEN: Sept. 4, 1999

RESULT: New York Liberty win game two of the 1999 WNBA Finals

WHAT: Teresa Weatherspoon's last-second miracle is known as "The Shot"—not just the most famous shot in WNBA history, but also the league's most famous moment. Her half-court heave went off the backboard and gave the New York Liberty a game two win over the dominant Houston Comets. In 1999, the WNBA Finals were best of three, so the crowd at the Toyota Center was standing, anticipating a celebration. The Comets were about to win their third consecutive W title. Instead, Weatherspoon—off one foot, just before the half-court line, and with a defender right there—did the unthinkable. In the second after, she sat on the court, and her teammates mobbed her. "Thank God," Weatherspoon told NBC just minutes later. "I knew it was good. Soon as it left my hand, it just looked as if it was good, and I was just praying that it went in."

PLAYER: Nneka Ogwumike

TIME LEFT ON CLOCK: 3.1 seconds

WHEN: Oct. 20, 2016

RESULT: Wins Los Angeles the 2016 WNBA title

WHAT: In the decisive game five of the W Finals, on the Minnesota Lynx home floor, the Sparks had the ball with fifteen seconds left. Even before this moment, the game had been a back-and-forth. Big-time shots had been swapped. Candace Parker had put Los Angeles up with 19.7 seconds left. Then Maya Moore dropped a turnaround jumper on the baseline to give the Lynx the lead. After Moore's heroics, the Sparks were in a hurry. They had no timeouts left. Guard Chelsea Gray took the inbounds pass and drove the length of the floor, missing a fadeaway jumper with about seven seconds left. Ogwumike snagged the offensive rebound, but her first attempt was blocked by Sylvia Fowles. Ogwumike grabbed the ball again and, fading away along the baseline, hit a jumper with 3.1 seconds remaining. The title was Los Angeles's third.

PLAYER: Morgan William

TIME LEFT ON CLOCK: At the buzzer in OT

WHEN: March 31, 2017

RESULT: Mississippi State beats UConn in 2017 NCAA semis, ends 111-game win streak

WHAT: In the final timeout, Mississippi State coach Vic Schaefer looked at William. "Mo, you about to win the game." The game was tied 64–64, which was a miracle to begin with. The Connecticut Huskies hadn't lost a game in years: 111 straight. But the Bulldogs had the ball and a chance, and with about four seconds left, William caught a pass at the top of the key. "Time was ticking," William said after. "I knew the last—end of regulation, I went for a layup, they blocked it. I was like, 'She probably think I'm going to do it again.'" Instead, William faked a pass inside, then quickly dribbled to the right elbow and launched a jumper over the defender's outstretched arm.

PLAYER: Kristi Toliver

TIME LEFT ON THE CLOCK: 6.1 seconds

WHEN: April 4, 2006

RESULT: Sends 2006 NCAA title game to OT, Maryland wins title

WHAT: The Maryland Terrapins called a timeout and diagrammed a play to put the ball into the hands of guard Kristi Toliver. They were down three points to favored Duke, 70–67, and Maryland coach Brenda Frese knew Toliver was her best bet. The quick guard caught the sideline inbounds pass, then drove off consecutive on-ball screens to the right wing. Toliver noticed that on the second screen a post player, six-foot-seven-inch Alison Bales, had switched onto her. So she faked a drive and stepped back behind the line, launching the game-tying shot. The post defender was so close that Toliver could feel her fingertips scrape her wrist. "One of the most pressure situations you could ever face as a young player," Frese said afterward.

PLAYER: Alana Beard

TIME ON CLOCK: At the buzzer

WHEN: Oct. 9, 2016

RESULT: Los Angeles Sparks win game one of the 2016 WNBA Finals

WHAT: Near half-court, Los Angeles point guard Chelsea Gray dribbled down the clock with the game tied, 76–76. Our eventual hero, Alana Beard, was camped out in the right corner. Gray came off a screen at the top of the key, penetrated, and kicked out to Beard as the clock ran down. The opening game of the Finals had been nip-and-tuck all the way: nineteen ties and ten lead changes. But at the buzzer, Beard—who was known as a defensive specialist—hit from deep, and the Sparks stole game one on the Lynx's home floor.

PLAYER: Maya Moore

TIME ON CLOCK: At the buzzer

WHEN: Oct. 9, 2015

RESULT: The Minnesota Lynx win game three of the 2015 WNBA Finals over the Indiana Fever

WHAT: The move is a study of efficiency. In just 1.7 seconds, Maya Moore catches the ball, pump fakes, takes one dribble to the right to create room, then rises for a textbook jumper. The Lynx had possession of the ball along their own sideline, the game tied at 77, when Lynx guard Lindsay Whalen hit Moore with the pass at the top of the key. "I think my natural state is to go really fast," Moore told reporters right after. "That's just my personality. Go really fast, play really hard, and ask questions later."

PLAYER: Diana Taurasi

TIME ON CLOCK: 14.3 seconds

WHEN: Sept. 12, 2014

RESULT: Phoenix Mercury sweep Chicago Sky for 2014 WNBA title

WHAT: Diana Taurasi has scored the most points in WNBA Finals history. And on this possession, she added a couple more. The game was tied, and the Mercury had the ball. It was in Taurasi's hands, and she would never relinquish it. She drove baseline with about nineteen seconds left on the game clock, planted her left foot and made a running fourteen-footer, absorbing contact from her defender and getting the and-one call. Her momentum would take her out of bounds, where she repeatedly pounded her chest. The move was a nod to her childhood idol-turned-friend, Kobe Bryant.

PLAYER: Sophia Young

TIME ON CLOCK: At the buzzer

WHEN: Sept. 27, 2008

RESULT: San Antonio Stars win game two of 2008 WNBA West Finals

WHAT: The Los Angeles Sparks appeared Finals-bound. They were one defensive play—and one second—from winning the West Finals. But the Silver Stars had possession along the sideline. And they boasted a lineup capable of a quick score, specifically guard Becky Hammon, who seemed ready to receive the inbounds pass and take the last-second shot. But the Sparks denied Hammon the ball. Instead, the ball went to forward Sophia Young. She caught it just inside the three-point line with a defender on her back. She immediately spun over her right shoulder and—at an odd angle—banked it off the glass. The Stars went on to win game three and advance to the franchise's first-ever WNBA Finals.

PLAYER: Deanna Nolan

TIME ON CLOCK: 53 seconds

WHEN: Sept. 16, 2003

RESULT: Detroit Shock win the 2003 WNBA Finals

WHAT: The shot was pure—straight through the net. A corner three from the explosive and perpetually underrated Deanna Nolan that put the Shock ahead of the Sparks for good. The shot was magic, but the circumstances elevate the moment to iconic. The Los Angeles Sparks were gunning for their third consecutive title. Everyone figured the Sparks would win another. Everyone except the upstart Shock and the sellout crowd of 22,076 who packed the Palace at Auburn Hills. (Still the most fans to *ever* attend a W game.) The season before, Detroit had been the worst team in the league, making Nolan's jumper all the more improbable.

PLAYER: Nikki Teasley

TIME ON CLOCK: 2.1 seconds

WHEN: Aug. 31, 2002

RESULT: Los Angeles Sparks win 2002 WNBA Finals

WHAT: Inside the Staples Center, against the New York Liberty, the Sparks were tied 66–66 with thirteen seconds left. The game was being aired by NBC: two of the founding franchises, anchored in key cities, dueling for a WNBA championship. The Sparks had the ball and it seemed likely they would go to superstar center Lisa Leslie or Mwadi Mabika. Rookie guard Nikki Teasley took the inbounds pass and seemed ready to dish off. But everyone was covered. Even Teasley's own defender, Teresa Weatherspoon, dropped off her. With no other options, Teasley rose and nailed the game-winner. It was the second consecutive title for Los Angeles.

THE MOMENT(S)

The Twelve Most Iconic Moments in Basketball History

(NOT ALREADY REFERENCED WITHIN)

WHEN: August 4, 2010

WHO: President Obama and Sasha Obama

WHAT: The then-president was known to be a hoops junkie, routinely playing pickup for his daily workout and flashing a smooth, left-handed stroke. Midway through his second term, President Obama and his youngest daughter sat courtside to watch the Washington Mystics play the Tulsa Shock. Sasha Obama even wore the jersey of Mystics' guard Alana Beard. For generations, presidents had made a point to attend important sports events, from the World Series to the Olympics. This was the first time a sitting American president attended a WNBA game.

2

WHEN: Present

WHO: Sabrina Ionescu and Steph Curry

WHAT: A crossover mentor-mentee relationship that reflects the growing camaraderie between the men's and women's games. Ionescu grew up in Northern California, where Curry was winning championships with the Golden State Warriors. The pair connected. And after Kobe Bryant's death in early 2020, they've grown even closer. The two FaceTimed after her WNBA debut, going over the game film. And they text regularly. "It's pretty awesome to know that, obviously, after his tragic death, that that connection grew even stronger with me and her, just in terms of the opportunity to take what Kobe was doing and what his legacy will continue to do in the women's game and carry that torch," Curry told *Sports Illustrated*.

rebound and outlet pass in a game against the Miami Sol, Leslie became the first woman to dunk in WNBA history. She repeated the feat in 2005. Since then, six players have dunked in W games: Michelle Snow, Candace Parker, Sylvia Fowles, Brittney Griner, Jonquel Jones, and Liz Cambage. (Griner has thrown down the most dunks in league history.)

WHEN: December 21, 1984

WHO: Georgeann Wells

WHAT: Wells became the first woman to dunk in an NCAA game. But, for decades, the proof was only in the eyewitness accounts and a singular photo by the communications staff at West Virginia, for whom Wells played. The only camera recording the momentous play belonged to the head coach of the opposition, Bud Francis. Finally, in 2009, on the twenty-fifth anniversary of the play, a *Wall Street Journal* reporter tracked down Francis's son and finally got his hands on the tape. "There was a chance for her to be on the *Today* show but some world event happened

WHEN: October 1998

WHO: Chamique Holdsclaw and *SLAM*

WHAT: 'Mique was a rising senior at the University of Tennessee when this iconic cover dropped. She had just led the Lady Vols to their third consecutive NCAA title and was the first woman to be featured solo on the magazine's cover. Because she's from Queens, New York, the jersey—and the head cocked sideways—translated perfectly. "We tried different things, and then I remember them breaking out the Knicks jersey," she told the magazine years later. "Next thing I know, it's like, 'Is the NBA ready for Chamique Holdsclaw?' It was a statement piece: Women's basketball had arrived."

WHEN: July 30, 2002

WHO: Lisa Leslie

WHAT: Leslie's epic career is peppered with firsts. She, alongside Sheryl Swoopes and Rebecca Lobo, were the first three cornerstone pieces of the WNBA. She was the first W player to reach 3,000 career points. And off a long

7

WHEN: 1985–86

WHO: University of Texas Longhorns and coach Jody Conradt

WHAT: Star freshman Clarissa Davis and the balanced Texas Longhorns became the first undefeated team in NCAA history. They finished 34–0 and defeated the University of Southern California and icon Cheryl Miller in the NCAA title game. Davis, who would go on to represent Team USA in 1992, scored thirty-two points in the semifinals and twenty-four points in the finals. "The first thought was perfection," Jody Conradt, the legendary coach, told reporters at the time. "There will be a champion crowned every year, but the undefeated champions will form an elite group." Conradt was right. Only three other programs have become undefeated champions: Tennessee, UConn (six times), and Baylor.

and she didn't get on," recalled Sharon Poe, West Virginia's communication officer. "This was something new for women's basketball, and it was somebody new, not a player from Tennessee or one of the power schools."

6

WHEN: 1987, 2011, 2021

WHO: The Game

WHAT: A year after the NCAA instituted the three-point line in men's college basketball, the arc was introduced to the women's game. The distance was set at 19 feet, 9 inches. The line stayed at that distance until 2011, when it was moved back to 20 feet, 9 inches. Then, before the 2021 season, the line moved to where it currently sits: 22 feet, 1¾ inches. When it was first introduced, the three-point line was seen as a gimmick—on both the men's and women's side—but it's now something most players couldn't imagine *not* existing.

the Game

 8

WHEN: April 4, 1993

WHO: Sheryl Swoopes

WHAT: In front of a sold-out arena, and on national TV, Swoopes single-handedly delivered a national championship to Texas Tech. She scored forty-three points as the Red Raiders upset Ohio State. It was Texas Tech's first national title in any sport and launched Swoopes as a household name. She was sixteen of twenty-four from the field and eleven of eleven from the free throw line. And the total was the most-ever scored in an NCAA final (men's or women's). "There are no words to explain what a great player Sheryl Swoopes is," said Texas Tech coach Marsha Sharp afterward. "We are just pleased that she got to show the whole nation."

9

WHEN: 1994

WHO: NCAA tournament field

WHAT: The number of programs included in the NCAA tournament has steadily increased since the NCAA first started running a women's tournament. From 1982—the first-ever tournament—until 1985 there were thirty-two teams. (For one season, in 1983, there were thirty-six.) Then from 1986 to 1988 the number increased to forty teams and was upped again to forty-eight teams for the next four seasons. Finally, in 1994, the field expanded to sixty-four teams. (The men's tournament had grown to sixty-four teams in 1985.) The most recent expansion came in 2021, when the tournament added four play-in games, bringing the total number of teams involved to sixty-eight.

10

WHEN: 1996

WHO: WNBA

WHAT: As the NBA conceived of the WNBA, and ideas about what it should be were bounced around, no one wanted to do anything gimmicky. But they wanted to separate the women's game visually. And so, they landed on the idea of differentiating the ball: alternating sections of the traditional orange with oatmeal. It was a marketing move. Here, former NBA commissioner David Stern explains his thinking: "One of the things that was insisted upon is we would have regular basketball uniforms. We weren't going to sexualize the players. And I remember conversations about the basketball itself. I think I take responsibility for saying we didn't want the WNBA ball to be in a store and look the same as other balls. So we decided on the oatmeal and orange colors."

WHEN: 1925, 1993

WHO: Iowa Girls High School Athletic Union
(IGHSAU)

WHAT: In 1925, at a meeting at a Presbyterian church in Des Moines, Iowa, the organization that oversaw high school athletics activities decided that it no longer wanted to sponsor girls' basketball. They claimed the game was "too strenuous" for young women. One high school superintendent, John W. Agans, disagreed and remarked, "Gentlemen, if you attempt to do away with girls' basketball in Iowa, you'll be standing at the center of the track when the train runs over you!" A group of men agreed with Agans, and they broke off and created a separate governing body, the IGHSAU, which would sponsor girls' state championships in Iowa beginning the following year. The tournament became wildly popular, routinely drawing thousands of fans each year. The Iowa game was six-on-six and remained that way until 1993, when the final six-on-six state championship was played between Hubbard-Radcliffe High School and Atlantic High School.

WHEN: 1957

WHO: US national team

WHAT: Many of the same players who helped the US to its first-ever world title in 1953 returned for the FIBA World Championships of 1957, which were held in Rio de Janeiro, Brazil. Players such as Rita Alexander, Joan Crawford, Barbara Ann Sipes, and Katherine "Katy" Washington were joined by Nera White and Alberta Cox. At the 1957 tournament, at Maracana Stadium in Rio de Janeiro, a capacity crowd of 40,000 watched the first-ever meeting between the US and the Soviet Union. Both teams were 5–0 in the tournament. The Soviets were the favorites, a European powerhouse who'd won the four previous European championships. But in the final seconds, on a free throw and added bucket at the end, the US prevailed in Brazil, 51–48. White was tournament MVP and Sipes scored eighteen points against the Soviets. The US wouldn't beat the Soviets again until 1986.

THE ALL-TIMERS

The Eight Most Iconic Figures in Basketball History

(NOT ALREADY REFERENCED WITHIN)

Ora Washington

TEAM: Germantown Hornets and Philadelphia Tribunes

Washington was enshrined in the Naismith Hall of Fame in 2018. She was, arguably, the greatest women's player of the Black Fives Era. She was born in Virginia in 1898, and her family, as part of the Great Migration, traveled north to Philadelphia. Washington, who was also a national tennis champion, first played for the Germantown Hornets. In 1932 she joined the Philadelphia Tribunes. The team barnstormed the country and won eleven consecutive Women's Colored Basketball World Championships, and Washington was the standout performer.

Hazel Walker

TEAM: Hazel Walker's Arkansas Travelers

When Walker first started playing at Ashdown High School in Arkansas in the early 1930s, the court was divided into thirds and players couldn't leave their sections. Arkansas didn't hold a state tournament for high schools, but the Amateur Athletic Union did. Walker went on to play for the Tulsa Business College. Her scholarship covered tuition, but she worked at a soda fountain to pay for room and board. After college, and for more than a decade, Walker played with numerous AAU teams and was named All-American eleven of her fourteen seasons. In 1946, Walker started playing for the All-American Red Heads, a professional traveling team. After three seasons, she broke

off and started her own barnstorming squad, Hazel Walker's Arkansas Travelers. The team played men's teams with men's rules. Walker played until she was fifty-one years old.

Sue Gunter

TEAMS: Nashville Business College, Middle Tennessee, Stephen F. Austin, Louisiana State University

Gunter almost single-handedly bridged the gap between the decades of AAU competition and the modern post–Title IX college game. Gunter played with Nera White at Nashville Business College, one of the iconic AAU teams, and also in international competition with the US national team in the early 1960s. She began her coaching career at Middle Tennessee at the end of her playing days, and act two of Gunter's basketball career was epic. When she retired in 2004 after twenty-two years at LSU, Gunter was the third-winningest coach—behind only Pat Summitt and Jody Conradt—in women's college basketball history.

Marian Washington

TEAMS: West Chester State College, University of Kansas

Almost everything about Marian Washington's career broke new ground. In 1969, she led West Chester State College to what is considered the first-ever college national championship. The game was sponsored by the Commission for Intercollegiate Athletics for Women (CIAW). In 1971, she was one of the first two Black athletes—along with Colleen Bowser—to play for the US national team. The next year, Washington became an assistant coach for Kansas and was elevated to head coach in 1973. She broke the color barrier for Division I women's basketball coaching. She stayed at Kansas for more than thirty years, won 560 games, and served as assistant coach for the iconic 1996 US national team that won Olympic gold.

Nera White

TEAM: Nashville Business College

Many insiders consider White the best basketball player they've ever seen. She was six foot one and could dunk, but could also pass and shoot from the outside. Longtime LSU coach Sue Gunter, who played with White on the AAU team at Nashville Business College, said of her teammate, "I've coached two Olympic teams and I've seen the best players in the world. Nera White is the best of them all." Before the existence of the AIAW or the NCAA, or any subsequent professional league, the game was run by the Amateur Athletic Union. White was named an AAU All-American for fifteen consecutive years, 1955–1969, and she led Nashville Business College to the AAU national title ten times during that stretch.

5

Kay Yow

TEAM: North Carolina State University, US national team

The modern women's game is a direct result of the pioneering work of coaches like Kay Yow. She was born in North Carolina. She was introduced to the game by her mother, who played for the local mill team. Yow and her sisters would play in the backyard. She played at East Carolina University, then coached high school for five years. Before Title IX reshaped college basketball, Yow became one of the game's first great coaches, for five seasons at Elon College, then long-term at North Carolina State. Yow was passionate and fierce. She was a president and founding member of the Women's Basketball Coaches Association (WBCA) and won an Olympic gold as head coach of the 1988 US national team.

Basketball Professional League (WBL). In addition to inventing the women's ball used by the WBL, Logan is famous for beating NBA legend Jerry West at H-O-R-S-E on the 1975 show *Battle of the Sexes*.

Bertha Teague

TEAM: Byng High School in Carthage, Missouri

In 1986, Teague was one of the first three women inducted into the Naismith Hall of Fame, alongside Senda Berenson Abbott (the "mother of basketball") and Margaret Wade (the "mother of college basketball"). Teague was known as "Mrs. Basketball of Oklahoma" and coached Byng High School to 1,157 wins across forty-three years. Her teams won eight state titles. Her sphere of influence extended far and included establishing coaching associations, serving on the national rules committee, and innovating on apparel. She was an early advocate for expanding the movement within the women's game—at a time when many rules restricted players to thirds of the court or even boxes. She championed the "unlimited dribble," and Oklahoma became the first state to adopt the rule. Coach Teague is a member of every basketball hall of fame for which she is eligible.

Karen Logan

TEAMS: All-American Red Heads, Indianapolis Pink Panthers, Chicago Hustle

A little-known fact: some people credit Karen Logan with inventing the slightly smaller women's basketball. Supposedly, she sold the idea to Wilson (without a lawyer) and the rest is history. Logan came of age in the 1950s and '60s playing in the neighborhood with the boys, but found herself in a time and location (California) where opportunities for girls were nonexistent. She attended Pepperdine University before athletic opportunities existed, then joined the barnstorming All-American Red Heads in the late 1960s. She stayed with them for a number of years before joining the semi-pro Pink Panthers. In 1978, she played for the Chicago Hustle of the newly formed Women's

THE TEAM(S)

The Five Most Iconic Teams

(NOT ALREADY REFERENCED WITHIN)

 WAYLAND BAPTIST FLYING QUEENS (1940s-PRESENT): Decades before women's college athletics became vogue, a tiny school in West Texas was far ahead of its time. The Flying Queens of Wayland Baptist played on athletic scholarships, traveled by private plane, and even borrowed fancy warm-up drills from the Harlem Globetrotters. From 1953 to 1958 the squad won 131 consecutive games. To place that in cultural perspective, as the *New York Times* writes, the streak "began early in the first term of the Eisenhower administration, remained aloft as McDonald's golden arches first appeared...then fell from orbit two months after *Sputnik*." The team won ten national titles (AAU). "That culture was almost a dichotomy," former Wayland player Courtney Donaldson told the *New York Times* of playing in Texas during the 1950s. "On one hand, it was 'Sit in the back row and keep your mouth shut.' On the other hand, it was liberal enough to allow women to participate in basketball and be successful."

 PHILADELPHIA TRIBUNES (1930-1944): This squad dominated the game, winning eleven consecutive Women's Colored Basketball World Championships before racial integration. The team was once named the Quick Steppers, but star Inez Patterson proposed a naming rights deal to the *Philadelphia Tribune*—the famous Black newspaper—and the paper accepted. The Quick Steppers became the Tribunes and soon Ora Washington joined from their intra-city rival, the Germantown Hornets. For more than a decade, the *Tribune* (the newspaper) provided the team financial stability and advertising and promotion. The team frequently toured, bringing the game to the South. As the country became embroiled in World War II, and the team's patron at the newspaper died, the Tribunes disbanded.

 HANES HOSIERY (1945-1954): During this era, the top women's players competed on AAU teams that were mostly affiliated with businesses, though some with colleges. The women who played for Hanes Hosiery also worked for the company. But head coach Virgil Yow also recruited great players to come play, and work. In 1953, the *Winston-Salem Journal and Sentinel* ran the headline, "Hosiery Wins Third Straight National Cagers Crown." It was the seventy-sixth of 102 consecutive victories for Hanes. And the team boasted stars Lurlyne Greer, Eunies Futch, and Eckie Jordan, all of whom would win a gold medal at the 1955 Pan America Games playing for the US team. Hanes—yes, the iconic underwear brand—disbanded the team in 1954, breaking the hearts of many of its players.

THE WOMEN WHO PLAYED FOR HANES HOSIERY ALSO WORKED FOR THE COMPANY.

 4

TEXAS COWGIRLS (1949–1977): The Cowgirls were started and run by legendary promoter Dempsey Hovland, and the team played more than 5,000 games in its history—most of them against men. The Cowgirls were also racially integrated well ahead of their time and broke gender and racial barriers. Hovland also spun off another all-women barnstorming team, the New York Harlem Queens. In the 1950s, the Cowgirls opened for the legendary Harlem Globetrotters when Harlem had Wilt Chamberlain. The women would also often open for NBA teams, back when the league was still struggling to find its sea legs. Attending a Texas Cowgirls show was a jam-packed event: sometimes famed Negro league pitcher Satchel Paige toured with the squad and gave a pitching demonstration at halftime; sometimes, country star Hank Williams performed. The Cowgirls played as many as 150 games a year and traveled to places such as Spain and Africa.

 5

NASHVILLE BUSINESS COLLEGE (1930s–1969): When she was ninety-two years old, former NBC player Alline Banks Sprouse told the *Tennessean*, "Back then [playing] meant my life. It meant everything." To play for NBC was like playing for UConn, except without any of the perks. The team drove across country for games, changed in the basement of buildings, and donned flimsy canvas sneakers. It didn't matter. They were *playing*. And playing well. Although the model no longer exists, Nashville Business College only sponsored the team; players didn't necessarily have to be enrolled at the school and could play for as many years as they remained competitive. Most of the team's stars held down jobs while competing for AAU titles. And NBC would win eleven of them during its heyday, including eight consecutive from 1962 to 1969. Many future inductees to the Women's Basketball Hall of Fame played for NBC, including (among others) Nera White, Joan Crawford, Rita Horky, and Doris Rogers.

TO PLAY FOR NBC WAS LIKE PLAYING FOR UCONN.

THE W 25

Twenty-Five Players for Twenty-Five Years

(ALPHABETICAL ORDER) · *Illustrated by Arizona O'Neill*

1 Seimone Augustus

- Two-time Olympic gold medalist
- Four-time WNBA champion (Minnesota Lynx)
- Eight-time WNBA All-Star
- 2011 WNBA Finals MVP

3 Swin Cash

- Two-time Olympic gold medalist
- Three-time WNBA champion (Detroit Shock and Storm)
- Four-time WNBA All-Star
- 2009 and 2011 WNBA MVP

5 Tina Charles

- Three-time Olympic gold medalist
- Eight-time WNBA All-Star
- Four-time WNBA rebounding champion
- 2012 WNBA MVP

2 Sue Bird

- Five-time Olympic gold medalist
- Four-time WNBA champion (Seattle Storm)
- Thirteen-time WNBA All-Star
- WNBA all-time assist leader

4 Tamika Catchings

- Four-time Olympic gold medalist
- Ten-time WNBA All-Star
- Five-time WNBA Defensive Player of the Year
- 2012 WNBA champion (Indiana Fever)

6 Cynthia Cooper-Dyke

- 1988 Olympic gold medalist
- Four-time WNBA champion (Houston Comets)
- Four-time WNBA Finals MVP
- Three-time WNBA scoring champion

7 Elena Delle Donne

- 2016 Olympic gold medalist
- Six-time WNBA All-Star
- 2015 and 2019 WNBA MVP
- 2019 WNBA champion (Washington Mystics)

8 Sylvia Fowles

- Four-time Olympic gold medalist
- Eight-time WNBA All-Star
- Two-time WNBA champion (Lynx)
- 2017 WNBA MVP

9 Yolanda Griffith

- Two-time Olympic gold medalist
- Eight-time WNBA All-Star
- 1999 WNBA MVP
- 2005 WNBA champion (Sacramento Monarchs)

10 Brittney Griner

- Two-time Olympic gold medalist
- Eight-time WNBA All-Star
- Eight-time WNBA blocks leader
- 2014 WNBA champion (Phoenix Mercury)

11 Becky Hammon

- Six-time WNBA All-Star
- Two-time All-WNBA First Team
- 2007 WNBA assists leader

12 Lauren Jackson

- Three-time Olympic silver medalist (Australia)
- Seven-time WNBA All-Star
- Three-time WNBA champion (Seattle Storm)
- 2010 WNBA MVP

⑬ Lisa Leslie

- Four-time Olympic gold medalist
- Eight-time All-WNBA First Team
- Three-time WNBA MVP (2001, 2004, 2006)
- Two-time WNBA champion (Los Angeles Sparks)

⑭ Angel McCoughtry

- Two-time Olympic gold medalist
- Five-time WNBA All-Star
- Two-time WNBA scoring champion
- Seven-time WNBA All-Defensive First Team

⑮ Maya Moore

- Two-time Olympic gold medalist
- Four-time WNBA champion (Lynx)
- Five-time All-WNBA First Team
- 2014 WNBA MVP

⑯ Nneka Ogwumike

- Seven-time WNBA All-Star
- 2016 WNBA champion (Sparks)
- 2016 WNBA MVP
- Four-time WNBA All-Defensive First Team

⑰ Candace Parker

- Two-time Olympic gold medalist
- Two-time WNBA champion (Sparks, Chicago Sky)
- 2008 and 2013 WNBA MVP
- 2020 WNBA Defensive Player of the Year

⑱ Ticha Penicheiro

- Seven-time WNBA assists leader
- Four-time WNBA All-Star
- 2008 All-Defensive First Team
- 2005 WNBA champion (Monarchs)

⑲ Cappie Pondexter

- 2008 Olympic gold medalist
- Seven-time WNBA All-Star
- Two-time WNBA champion (Mercury)
- 2007 WNBA Finals MVP

㉑ Breanna Stewart

- Two-time Olympic gold medalist
- Two-time WNBA champion (Storm)
- 2018 WNBA MVP
- Two-time WNBA Finals MVP

㉓ Diana Taurasi

- Five-time Olympic gold medalist
- Three-time WNBA champion (Mercury)
- Ten-time All-WNBA First Team
- Five-time WNBA scoring champion

⑳ Katie Smith

- Three-time Olympic gold medalist
- Seven-time WNBA All-Star
- Two-time WNBA champion (Shock)
- 2008 WNBA Finals MVP

㉒ Sheryl Swoopes

- Three-time Olympic gold medalist
- Four-time WNBA champion (Comets)
- Three-time WNBA MVP
- Three-time WNBA Defensive Player of the Year

㉔ Tina Thompson

- Two-time Olympic gold medalist
- Four-time WNBA champion (Comets)
- Nine-time WNBA All-Star
- Three-time All-WNBA First Team

㉕ Lindsay Whalen

- Two-time Olympic gold medalist
- Four-time WNBA champion (Lynx)
- Five-time WNBA All-Star
- Three-time WNBA assists leader

OCEAN'S 5

The Best International Players of All Time

(NOT ON THE TOP TWENTY-FIVE LIST)

Illustrated by Arizona O'Neill

ULJANA SEMJONOVA: Lithuania/Soviet Union

HOMETOWN: Zarasai, Lithuanian SSR, Soviet Union

BORN: 1952

In the 1970s and 80s, Semjonova dominated international competition. She anchored the Soviet Union (then USSR) teams that won the Olympic gold medal in 1976 and 1980. She stands seven feet tall and in 1993 became the first non-US woman enshrined in the Basketball Hall of Fame.

LIZ CAMBAGE: Australia

HOMETOWN: Melbourne, Australia

BORN: 1991

A force in the middle, Cambage won an Olympic bronze medal with Australia in 2012. She was the number two overall pick in the 2011 WNBA draft and is a four-time WNBA All-Star. She currently plays for the Los Angeles Sparks.

PENNY TAYLOR: Australia

HOMETOWN: Melbourne, Australia

BORN: 1981

In 2022, Taylor was enshrined in the Women's Basketball Hall of Fame. She won two Olympic silver medals playing for Australia and was a three-time WNBA champion—and three-time W All-Star—during her career with the Phoenix Mercury.

MWADI MABIKA: Congo

HOMETOWN: Kinshasa, Zaire

BORN: 1976

Mabika came to the United States from the Congo (formerly known as Zaire) with the help of countryman (and NBA legend) Dikembe Mutombo. She played twelve seasons in the WNBA, eleven of them with the Los Angeles Sparks. She won two WNBA titles and was twice named a WNBA All-Star.

EMMA MEESSEMAN: Belgium

HOMETOWN: Ypres, West Flanders, Belgium

BORN: 1993

Meesseman, a power forward, has won a WNBA title with the Washington Mystics. She was the 2019 WNBA Finals MVP and has twice been named a W All-Star.

THE MOVIES THAT SHOULD HAVE BEEN

We Reimagine Hollywood over the Years

Illustrated by Louie Chin

1

Love & Basketball

WITH: Skylar Diggins-Smith

YEAR: 2000

STARRING: Phoenix Mercury guard Skylar Diggins-Smith

PLOT: Monica Wright (now played by Diggins-Smith) and Quincy McCall grow up next door to each other in Los Angeles. Both love the game and pursue their careers before fate brings them back together again.

2

She Got Game

WITH: Chamique Holdsclaw

YEAR: 1998

STARRING: University of Tennessee superstar Chamique Holdsclaw

PLOT: Eve Shuttlesworth is the best high school player in the country. Her mother is briefly paroled from prison to convince Eve to attend the alma mater of the governor in exchange for a reduced sentence.

3

Blue Chips

WITH: Lisa Leslie and Cynthia Cooper

YEAR: 1994

STARRING: Lisa Leslie and Cynthia Cooper at the University of Southern California

PLOT: The coach at USC (played by Helen Mirren) is forced to face the dark underbelly of college recruiting in order to stay competitive and lure the brightest high school stars.

Space Jam

WITH: Sheryl Swoopes

YEAR: 1996

STARRING: Sheryl Swoopes

PLOT: Swoopes, playing herself, teams up with a cast of characters to help them earn their freedom from an evil alien determined to export the cartoons to another planet.

Space Jam: A New Legacy

YEAR: 2021

STARRING: Las Vegas Aces all-star A'ja Wilson

PLOT: The reigning WNBA MVP, Wilson, must work with Bugs Bunny to win a basketball game after rogue artificial intelligence kidnaps Wilson's teammate.

White Women Can't Jump

WITH: Arike Ogunbowale and Marina Mabrey

YEAR: 1992

STARRING: Arike Ogunbowale and Marina Mabrey of the Dallas Wings

PLOT: Best friends Arike and Marina hustle on the basketball courts of South Bend, staying one step ahead of the mobsters they owe money to.

SKYLAR DiGGINS SMiTH

LOVE & BASKETBALL

BLUE CHIPS

CYNTHIA COOPER   LISA LESLIE

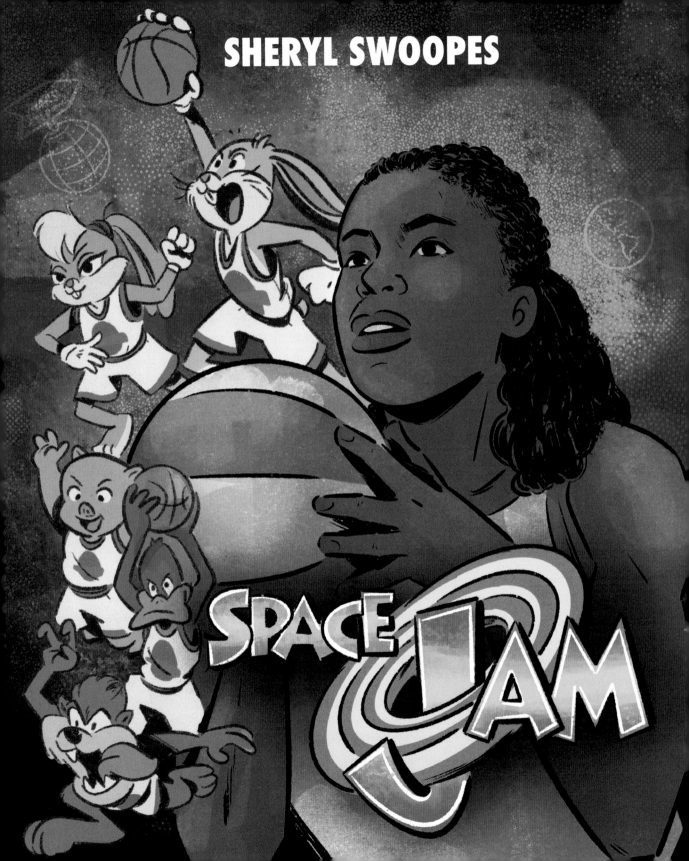

(W)NBA JAM

We Pair Together the Top Ten Dynamic Duos That Would Have Ruled the Video Game

When NBA Jam was first released in 1993, Sheryl Swoopes was dominating the women's college game at Texas Tech, just barely slipping past Katie Smith's Ohio State in the NCAA final. Way over in Europe, Cynthia Cooper was running the courts. And yet, none of these iconic women made it into the video game, which remains one of the most famous sports games ever made. Here, we rewrite (and re-illustrate!) history with a few of the dynamic duos that would have soared above the rest.

HARRIS

SPEED :
2PTRS :
3PTRS* : N/A
DEF. :

HAIRSTON

SPEED :
2PTRS :
3PTRS : N/A
DEF. :

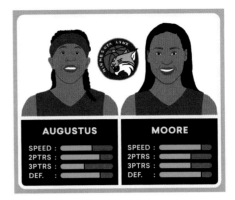

AUGUSTUS

SPEED :
2PTRS :
3PTRS :
DEF. :

MOORE

SPEED :
2PTRS :
3PTRS :
DEF. :

DONOVAN

SPEED :
2PTRS :
3PTRS : N/A
DEF. :

LIEBERMAN

SPEED :
2PTRS :
3PTRS* : N/A
DEF. :

SWOOPES

SPEED :
2PTRS :
3PTRS :
DEF. :

THOMPSON

SPEED :
2PTRS :
3PTRS :
DEF. :

JACKSON

SPEED :
2PTRS :
3PTRS :
DEF. :

BIRD

SPEED :
2PTRS :
3PTRS :
DEF. :

LOBO

SPEED :
2PTRS :
3PTRS :
DEF. :

WEATHERSPOON

SPEED :
2PTRS :
3PTRS :
DEF. :

JACKLYN JONES

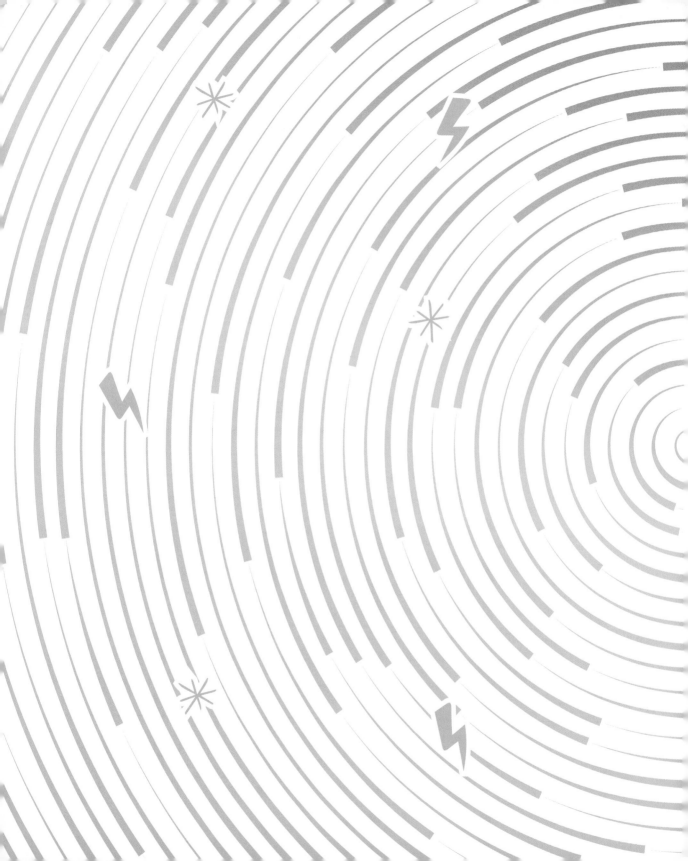

FINAL SCENE

THE RETURN

ARTWORK BY MILAN ABAD

Jacklyn opened her eyes. She was in the locker room again. She looked down at her hands, at the carpet, at the room around her. Yes, OK, she was back. Her head whipped around the room. Where was the older woman? Jacklyn stood and peered around the corner. Nothing. She was definitely alone again.

What had just happened? She felt like she'd been inside each moment in time. But that couldn't be possible. Maybe the woman possessed some fancy new upload for the metaverse, though Jacklyn had never experienced a game so real. She'd seen the wonder on the faces of the young women who first held a basketball—just a bulky leather thing, really—and the heat from their bodies as they played.

For the first time, she felt connected to all the women who'd played this game before her. All the stories buzzed inside her. How had she not known of the depth of their passion and pain? It had never been told before, that's why! Jacklyn sat in wonder for a moment. But then the familiar *ding* announcing that the locker room door had opened. Jacklyn sat up straight, expecting the elderly woman to walk into the room. When her teammate came around the corner, Jacklyn couldn't help but deflate a little.

"Who were you expecting, J?" her teammate kidded.

Still two hours to tip-off, Jacklyn realized. But she was buzzing with energy. She needed to get out on the court, feel the ball in her hands, find a state of meditation.

Outside the arena, New York City was lit up about that night's game. The newest skyscrapers pierced the sky, and Aeromobils were pulling into apartments on the highest floors. Down on the street, fans were milling outside the rebuilt Madison Square Garden, looking for tickets to be transferred to their wrist chips. The price was steep. But so many living legends would be inside the building, not to mention *the* Jacklyn Jones—hometown sensation! As soon as the doors opened, fans wearing W jerseys of all kinds—the Liberty, the Mercury, even the long-ago Houston Comets—poured through the doors.

FOR THE FIRST TIME, SHE FELT CONNECTED TO ALL THE WOMEN WHO'D PLAYED THIS GAME BEFORE HER.

Soon, tip-off was approaching, and the arena was filled to capacity. Jacklyn and her Liberty teammates jogged off the court and sat on the team bench. They watched as dozens of women, many of them walking with canes, filled the court. The WNBA had given each of them a hand-stitched jersey featuring the team they had played for, along with their last name on the back.

Jacklyn was riveted. She recognized so many of them. And now she knew their stories! She couldn't help herself. When she heard the announcer call, "Chamique Holdsclaw!" she popped off her chair and went to greet one of the greatest players of her generation, now so old but still with that gleam in her eye.

"What an honor," Jacklyn said, standing in front of Chamique. "The 'Three Meeks'— like the Beatles! Your pull-up jumper!"

Jacklyn turned and heard the announcer call out Arike Ogunbowale's name, and Jacklyn's mind flashed to that turnaround three-pointer at the buzzer, that long-ago Final Four.

"Clutch!" Jacklyn said, mimicking the move. "Thank you for everything."

She walked past Sue Bird and winked and said, "Bird at the Buzzer! Thank you for fighting for our game."

As she warmly embraced all the players she recognized—A'ja Wilson, Jonquel Jones, Elena Delle Donne—she thanked them. But Jacklyn was still looking for one former player in

THEY WATCHED AS DOZENS OF WOMEN, MANY OF THEM WALKING WITH CANES, FILLED THE COURT.

particular: the old woman in the orange hoodie. Finally, she saw the woman saluting the crowd as the announcer called her name: "Seimone Augustus!"

"How did you do it?" Jacklyn said as Seimone took her place.

"Gotta know where you come from, young one," Seimone said.

Around them, the crowd roared.

ACKNOWLEDGMENTS

The original idea for this book was born of joyful energy. "Wait, wouldn't it be so much fun if…?" was my first driving thought. And while I hope, and believe, we've created a book in keeping with that original spirit, the truth is that the pursuit quickly became serious. How could it not? Once I began poking around in our game's history, I realized how many women (and some men) had fought for the right to play, or who had laced 'em up despite the social risks—who had loved the game and nurtured it in every corner of our country (and beyond!). Everywhere I looked, I found new stories. And so, I began to see *Hoop Muses* as a way of sharing a lineage, connecting the dots, honoring women who have too-often been erased, their achievements dimmed. In that pursuit, I leaned heavily on the seminal work *Shattering the Glass* by Pamela Grundy and Susan Shackelford as well as *Full-Court Quest* by Linda S. Peavy and Ursula Smith. The writing of Mariah Burton Nelson was also invaluable. In addition, the Black Fives Foundation was crucial in piecing together the stories of Black club basketball in the early-to-mid twentieth century. Finally, a big thank-you to all the women who were willing to speak with me for this book: Ann Meyers, Charlotte Smith, Semeka Randall, Cheryl Miller, Lois Greenfield, Nancy Lieberman, Vanessa Nygaard, Jackie Stiles, Carol Stiff, Donna Lopiano, Debby Jennings, Mickie DeMoss, Holly Warlick, Cynthia Cooper, and Teresa Edwards.

This book wouldn't exist without the championing of Sean Desmond at Twelve, who saw our vision from the first moment and gave us the freedom (and time) to create the book of our dreams. Thank you also to the team at Twelve who provided invaluable support: First and foremost and forever, Zohal Karimy (long chats on the phone!), without whom this book would absolutely not exist as it does. Zoe—thank you for your tireless effort to bring this to life. Thanks also to Tareth Mitch and Nyamekye Waliyaya. The book's extraordinary designer, Laura Palese, did justice to Sophia Chang's dynamic illustrations and helped seamlessly tell this story. The supporting illustrators—Milan Abad, Louie Chin, and Arizona O'Neill—brought another dimension to the book: thank you all.

As always, my agent at CAA, Anthony Mattero: Thank you for receiving the original pitch for this idea and saying YES, YES, YES. I am so glad we get to work together. Thanks also to Lindsay Kagawa Colas at Wasserman. I remember calling my mom while out for a walk a few minutes after coming up with the idea for this book and she was giddy with the possibilities! She was there for every twist and turn of the *Hoop Muses* journey. Thanks, Mom! Kathryn and Ashi: I love you the most, the most.

I hope this book nimbly (and joyfully!) captures the history of our beautiful game.

—Kate

ABOUT THE AUTHORS AND ILLUSTRATOR

Kate Fagan is an Emmy Award–winning journalist and the number one *New York Times* best-selling author of *What Made Maddy Run*, as well as the coming-of-age memoir *The Reappearing Act*. Her third book, *All the Colors Came Out*, was released in May 2021 from Little, Brown. She currently works for Meadowlark Media and hosts the podcast *Off the Looking Glass*. She previously spent seven years as a columnist and feature writer for espnW, ESPN.com, and *ESPN The Magazine*. She lives in Charleston, South Carolina, with her wife, Kathryn Budig, and their two dogs.

Seimone Delicia Augustus (born April 30, 1984) is an American former professional basketball player who last played for the Los Angeles Sparks of the Women's National Basketball Association (WNBA), Dynamo Kursk, and the US national team. She was drafted by the Minnesota Lynx first overall in the 2006 WNBA draft, and left to sign with the Sparks fourteen years later. An eight-time all-star, Augustus has become one of the most recognizable faces in the WNBA, earning MVP honors while leading the Lynx to the 2011 WNBA championship, the first of four WNBA championships that she won with the Lynx.

Sophia Chang hails from the borough of Queens, New York, and in less than a decade managed to champion a name for herself in the art, design, and streetwear community worldwide. With her BFA from Parsons School of Design coupled with a natural acumen for business, she has collaborated with A-list names across multiple fields. Passionate about everyone's story, she listens and interprets those stories to empower the community she loves and respects. Sophia is a creative engine who lives to propel her friends and clients to greatness.

Twelve
Hachette Book Group
1290 Avenue of the Americas, New York, NY 10104
twelvebooks.com
twitter.com/twelvebooks

First Edition: March 2023

Twelve is an imprint of Grand Central Publishing. The Twelve name
and logo are trademarks of Hachette Book Group, Inc.

The publisher is not responsible for websites (or their content) that
are not owned by the publisher.

The following artwork is by Milan Abad: Full-page illustrated openers on pages 6 and
251, and comic strips on pages 7, 16, 29, 39, 60, 75, 95, 107, 123, 127, 167, 207, 217, and 251.

Artwork on pages 232-237 is by April O'Neill. Artwork on pages 240-245 is by
Louis Chin. All other artwork is by Sophia Chang.

The Hachette Speakers Bureau provides a wide range of authors for speaking
events. To find out more, go to www.hachettespeakersbureau.com or
call (866) 376-6591.

Library of Congress Cataloging-in-Publication Data
Names: Augustus, Seimone, 1984- author. | Fagan, Kate (Sports writer)
author. | Chang, Sophia, illustrator.
Title: Hoop muses : an insider's guide to pop culture and the (women's)
game / Seimone Augustus and Kate Fagan ; [illustrated by Sophia Chang].
Description: First edition | New York, N.Y. : Twelve, 2023.
Identifiers: LCCN 2022047925 | ISBN 9781538709146 (hardcover) |
ISBN 9781538709160 (ebook)
Subjects: LCSH: Basketball for women—United States—History. | Women
basketball players—United States—Biography.
Classification: LCC GV886 .A94 2023 | DDC 796.323082—dc23/eng/20221103
LC record available at https://lccn.loc.gov/2022047925

ISBNs: 978-1-5387-0914-6 (hardcover); 978-1-5387-0916-0 (ebook)

Printed in the United States of America

WOR

10 9 8 7 6 5 4 3 2 1